BORN TO STARVE

JOSEPH D. TYDINGS

BORN TO STARVE

WILLIAM MORROW & COMPANY, INC.
New York 1970

I dedicate this book to my grandfather, the late Ambassador Joseph E. Davies, who was everything a grandfather could be and more, who inspired and encouraged me to the public service from my earliest days and who is "up on a cloud cheering his only grandson on."

Foreword

NO crisis faced by human beings in the four million or so years our species has walked the earth has ever approached the magnitude of the population-resource-environment crisis which is now upon us. Skyrocketing numbers of human beings, inadequate food resources, disappearing mineral resources, and deterioration of the ecological systems upon which all human life depends are combining in a series of interactions which pose a mortal threat to every man, woman, and child on the planet. The increasing threats of thermonuclear war, world-wide plague, and massive famine are all part and parcel of this crisis, as are such relatively less perilous phenomena as our decaying cities, the deterioration of the American educational system, the plight of minorities, and so forth. All knowledgeable observers agree that the entire world system—and it must be viewed as a unitary system—is running downhill at an astonishing rate. We will be fortunate indeed if civilization persists to the end of this century.

If mankind is to be saved, an unprecedented change of human attitudes will be required. It is especially important that politicians in the United States—the most powerful nation in the world—recognize the true dimensions of the problem, and take direct action to ameliorate the crisis. The United States must set an example by adopting firm policies of population control and starting to convert from a wasteful, polluting, "cowboy" economy to a "spaceman" economy which emphasizes the quality of life and the husbanding of resources. Once we have started on that road, we may be able to persuade other overdeveloped countries to do the same. We may then ask them to join us in a crash program to help the underdeveloped countries to control their population and to semidevelop. Semidevelopment would provide these countries with a quality agrarian life, providing adequate food, housing and medical care, as well as a reasonable supply of manufactured goods supplied by the industrial countries. It would be a task of unprecedented difficulty, but the rewards of success would also be unprecedented.

At a time when many politicians are mouthing empty phrases about "ecology" and "environment," and busily ignoring the population problem, Americans can take cheer from the knowledge that our legislature contains a small but determined band of men who do understand the problem. This fine book is by one of the most knowledgeable of them. I hope it will be read by all Americans who are interested in survival.

Paul R. Ehrlich
Department of Biological Sciences
Stanford University,
Stanford

Contents

Introduction

AT 10:56 P.M. on July 24, 1969, as perhaps a billion earth men and women listened and watched, Neil Armstrong became the first human to set foot on another heavenly body. Poised alone against the stark lunar landscape, Armstrong provided a dramatic symbol of the ingenuity and courage man has demonstrated in his unceasing struggle to master nature.

However, quieter, less prepossessing events back on this planet raised the grim prospect that the spectacular staged in the Sea of Tranquility was not the "dawn of a new era" many proclaimed, that it was merely an ironic footnote to the story of man's tragic destruction of his earthly environment and, ultimately, of himself.

During the eight-day mission of Apollo 11, the population of the world increased by more than one and one-half million human beings—a rate of 192,000 more people each day, 76 million a year. Over this same eight-day period, an estimated 100,000 human beings starved to death—most of them children.

These figures, aggregated and projected, comprise the statistical dimensions of a population explosion unprecedented in human history. A doubling of the earth's inhabitants every thirty-five years which, if unchecked, will mean the mass starvation of hundreds of millions of people, the poisoning of our environment, and very possibly the destruction of the human race and the death of the planet.

Thus the macabre irony. For if we fail to devise a successful population policy on a global and national scale immediately, history may well record that man's flight to the stars occurred at the same moment he lost control of the mundane forces that threatened to destroy him.

This book is about the population explosion and the millions of people already caught in this demographic trap. It is the story of the wretched masses of the developing nations doomed to poverty, despair, and starvation as population growth outdistances food supplies and other critical resources. It is a plea for the millions of stunted and retarded children with distended stomachs and unhealing sores who will never reach adulthood, for the poor of our own urban and rural slums who are condemned to the economic and social backwaters of American society by our failure to provide them with the means to plan their families.

Finally, it is an attempt to mobilize concerned Americans to demand that their government devote the energy and resources needed to develop an effective national and worldwide population policy before it is too late.

Population is an issue which concerned me even before my election to the United States Senate in 1964. However, it took a trip to South America in December of 1967 to transform an intellectual awareness into the personal feelings of indignation and urgency this problem demands and deserves. There is something about the sight of starving children fighting with black crabs for garbage in the mud flats of a teeming slum that moves men in a manner no set of statistics can.

On my return to this country, I began talking about the imminent threat to man's survival posed by the growing gap between people and food whenever I found groups willing to listen.

In the spring of 1968, I was invited to deliver a commencement address at Green Mountain College in Poultney, Vermont. The title of the address was "Population and Mass Starvation." The emphasis was along the lines developed in this book, only, of course, in an abbreviated form.

The response was startling and gratifying. Students, parents, and faculty all commented that the address had made a tremendous impression on them. One of the parents was Howard Cady, an editor for the publishing house of William Morrow and Company. He urged me to give serious consideration to developing the theme of my commencement address into a book. This is the result.

No public servant has enough time in the day to devote himself to the amount of reading, writing, and contemplative thinking he would like to engage in. I am certainly no exception. A senator must rely on dedicated individuals who work in various specialties and have the facts, experience, and breadth of vision to supply the information on which wise policy decisions must be based. Preparation of the materials of this book has involved considerable time and effort on the part of many persons.

My respect and appreciation go to the innumerable researchers, professors, government employees, and private citizens who in very important ways contributed to the body of information contained here. To a great extent, it is their facts, their voices, their pleas that I offer for public discussion. Though others contributed greatly to the development of the facts and issues which are presented, I take sole responsibility for the material, for the way it is presented, and for any shortcomings that may exist.

I am most particularly grateful to my research assistant, Gerald Fill, for his considerable assistance and guidance in the assembly and preparation of the material on which this book is based. His persistence and intelligent grasp of the complex issues which comprise the population problem proved invaluable.

Similarly, the assistance of Douglas Ross, my legislative assistant, has been excellent. In addition to reviewing the original drafts and making cogent suggestions, he and Mr. Fill performed the basic staff work in translating my general concerns into the specific legislative proposals of S. 2108. This bill, which I introduced in the 91st Congress, now has eighty-seven co-sponsors in the House of Representatives and the Senate.

In addition, my appreciation and thanks go to Howard Cady for his inspiration, encouragement, and advice; Harry Mileham for his careful and objective editorial review and critique of the initial manuscript drafts; Dr. John Aird for his invaluable assistance with the China discussion; Dr. Irene Taeuber for her thoughtful advice on Asia; Dr. Erven Long for his review of the chapter on agricultural development; and the Legislative Reference Service of the Library of Congress for patiently compiling the many facts which form the core of this book. I particularly cite the able assistance I received from two Legislative Reference Service staff members, Mrs. Rieck Hannifin for her tireless assistance on the Latin America chapter and Miss Carolyn Colwell on the Africa chapter. Their contributions were vital.

The essence of a legislator's ability to carry out his duties effectively as a responsible public servant is the quality of his staff. I have been blessed with an especially dedicated, hard-working group of young men and women, who toil endlessly in Washington and Baltimore serving the public. They contributed considerably to the successful completion of this book. To Mrs. Mary Ernest, Mrs. Charlene Bess, Miss Vicki Dalton, Miss Nancy Granese, Miss Leslie Kohn, and Miss Nancy Dorman for patiently typing and retyping the many drafts of the manuscript, I offer special thanks.

Finally, this book would never have been possible without the patience and loyalty of my wife, Ginny, and our children.

Joseph D. Tydings

September, 1969

PART I

Dimensions
of the Problem

As a biologist, the human population explosion, and its declining spiral of natural resources, is to me the greatest threat of all. The time is ripe, even dangerously over-ripe, as far as the population control problem is concerned. We shall have to face up or ultimately perish, and what a dreary, stupid, unlovely way to perish, on a ruined globe stripped of its primeval beauty.

LOWELL SUMNER

I

The Time Bomb

MANKIND is breeding itself into oblivion. The earth is rapidly becoming too crowded. There are 3.5 billion people on the planet today. By the year 2000, that number is expected to double to 7 billion. Within the next decade or two, we will no longer possess the food and other resources needed to sustain so many people.

And this, simply stated, is what the population problem is all about.

It is a problem mankind has never confronted before on a global scale. Until very recently, the population of the planet increased at a leisurely pace. Historians estimate that eight thousand years ago, in that dimly understood period preceding the onset of recorded history, the human race consisted of a scant 5 million people scattered in tiny clusters across the face of the earth. With a death rate nearly equal to the birth rate, it had taken approximately a million years for the population to double from 2.5 million to that 5 million level.

Then a dramatic change took place—the agricultural revolution. People began to grow their food rather than hunt for it. Some of the risks inherent in the nomadic way of life were eliminated and the death rate dropped. The number of people on the planet began to double every thousand years. By A.D. 1650, only a few years after the Pilgrims landed at Plymouth, this plodding geometric process had boosted the earth's population to 500 million.

It was at this point, roughly three hundred years ago, that science and the nation-state combined to detonate the demographic explosion which is threatening us with disaster, and possibly extinction, today. The emergence of modern medicine and public sanitation and health programs sent death rates plummeting throughout much of the world. Infant and maternal mortality fell, life expectancy increased. Population "doubling time" dropped precipitously from one thousand years to two hundred years by 1850. It took only eighty years for the next doubling as the population reached 2 billion by 1930. Currently, the doubling time is 35 years. Were this rapid rate of population increase to persist for another six hundred years—an insignificant time span in man's million-year history—there would be one human being for every square foot of the earth's surface—land and sea!

Needless to say, such a world would hardly be a pleasant place to live; it might not even be livable at all. However, for better or worse, we will never have to contend with such a situation. Nature will not permit this "standing room only" condition to materialize.

Man's day of reckoning with this problem cannot be put off six hundred years, or even fifty years. Whether we wish it or not, the present imbalance between births and deaths will be redressed within our lifetimes. Either the nations of the world will act in time to defuse the population bomb with humane programs to sharply reduce birth rates, or Nature will ruthlessly restore the balance with her traditional culling tools of war, famine, and disease—the feared Horsemen of the Apocalypse. Either a birth rate solution or a death rate solution: the choice is still ours, though not for very long.

Currently, the road mankind is traveling terminates in a death rate solution.

What does this mean if nothing drastic is done to alter our course in the next few years? To begin with, it means that hundreds of millions of people surely will starve to death. Present food production is already inadequate. Roughly 2 billion people will go to bed tonight hungry and malnourished. According to conservative estimates, 3.5 million people will die of hunger in 1970; countless other millions undoubtedly will succumb to diseases after malnutrition has lowered their resistance.

What makes the outlook so bleak is the fact that the gap between mouths to feed and food is growing, not diminishing. In 1966, the population of the world jumped by 70 million people, but there was no equivalent increase in food production. Per-capita food supplies on the planet fell! In many parts of Latin America, this has been a recurring phenomenon throughout the 1960's. Over-all food production grows somewhat, but population grows as fast or faster.

Many of the developing nations of Asia, Africa, and Latin America must import foodstuffs each year to avert mass famine. However, the large agricultural surpluses from the United States, Canada, and Australia that bailed out India and other starving nations in the last decade are rapidly shrinking.

In 1966, the United States shipped one-quarter of its entire wheat crop to India. By 1976, India will have to feed 180 million *more* people. And it is unlikely America will have a sizable wheat surplus to help do the job.

So the pessimists predict terrible famine throughout most of the world by 1975 or 1980. The optimists point to an incipient agricultural revolution which promises new fecund varieties of wheat and rice. But even if this development results in a sharp rise in food production—and I pray it does—it does not represent a solution to the problem. At best, it will buy mankind an additional decade or two.

Unless birth rates fall dramatically, the moment of truth will surely arrive before the end of this century. It will not be a pretty sight. Within the next thirty years, we and our children will witness on television the agonizing death by starvation of millions upon millions of our fellow human beings. Biafra is an ominous portent of things to come. The world will be flooded with children—children with bloated bellies, misshapen limbs, and running sores—who literally are born to starve.

And starvation will not be the only guise assumed by the death rate solution. Indeed, the deterioration and destruction of our environment resulting from the population explosion threatens even more dire consequences for human survival than the growing food shortage. Mass famine means the death of millions of people. A poisoned environment may mean the death of mankind.

In our struggle to draw ever greater amounts of sustenance from the planet's limited arable lands, we have lost millions of acres of soil through exhaustion and erosion. When people are faced with starvation, intensive agricultural methods no doubt appear dictated by minimal standards of human decency.

Yet, one cannot forget the experience of earlier civilizations. The Fertile Crescent, that once plush and verdant Middle Eastern cradle of the great religions, has been transformed into a desert wasteland where nothing blooms. Men simply wore the land out.

Synthetic fertilizers and chemical pesticides employed to stretch food production to meet the needs of an exploding population are upsetting the ecological balance of large areas of the earth. Life forms such as insects, rodents, and birds are exterminated as pests. But nothing is substituted to fill their roles in the delicate system of checks and balances that nature has established to maintain life. The result: man creates dangerous new environmental problems for himself which require yet more chemicals and poisons to avert disaster.

And this artificially sustained life cycle may, in the long run, be lethal. There is growing evidence that these pesticides and insecticides are poisoning us. For example, we have contaminated virtually all of the animal systems of the world, including *Homo sapiens*, with DDT. Concentrations of DDT in the fat deposits of Americans average eleven parts per million. What are the ultimate physiological consequences of this contamination process? No one really seems to know. And as the struggle to raise more food intensifies, the prospect is for the increased use of these chemicals.

Great concentrations of people produced by our rapidly expanding population are also creating other forms of environmental pollution. A taxi driver in Manhattan today inhales exhaust and other combustion by-products equivalent to those obtained from smoking three packs of cigarettes a day. Those of us living or working in metropolitan areas are increasingly subject to diseases such as stroke, lung cancer, and emphysema whether we smoke or not. In short, our habits matter less. Our habitats are poisoning us.

The pollutants that are destroying the ecological balance on land are producing a similar effect in our rivers and lakes. Lake Erie is dead, a stinking cesspool in which little lives. Parts of the Potomac River are the same. Lake Michigan is following suit. Already, large cities throughout the world are experiencing water crises as fresh water supplies are exhausted or contaminated. The day is not distant when the lament of the Ancient Mariner will be universal.

Men are slowly awakening to the harsh reality that the resources on which they rely for survival are limited. We still lack a comprehensive resource inventory on which to plan the future. But one fact is inescapable. Our resources are not inexhaustible; if we continue to despoil and exploit them in a world whose population is doubling every thirty-five years, they will soon be depleted. If this happens, our legacy to our children will be a dying planet which offers them no future and no hope. And this is the direction we are headed toward today.

A third consequence of the death-rate-solution road on which we are currently traveling is continuing violence and unrest throughout the developing world. Liberty, equality, justice, "law and order" are empty shibboleths to a hungry man. Joseph Conrad wrote in *Heart of Darkness:* "No fear can stand up to hunger, no patience can wear it out, disgust simply does not exist where hunger is; and as to superstition, beliefs, and what you may call principles, they are less than chaff in a breeze."

If the current rates of population increase persist in the developing nations, their efforts to create viable, stable societies are doomed to failure. For population growth will continue to absorb increases in agricultural and industrial productivity, capital accumulation will remain impossible, and the resulting frustration of starving peoples without progress will erupt into desperate cycles of revolution and repression. Whatever our successes at home, we shall be condemned to live out our days in a hostile and dangerous environment in which poverty, despair, violence, and war remain the dominant themes.

This relationship between population and development constitutes a crucial dimension of the population problem, one to which the next chapter of the book is devoted. Sadly, it is a relationship that is too seldom discussed in deliberations over our foreign assistance and diplomatic policies.

These, then, are the probable results that our present "do nothing" attitude toward the population explosion will produce. These are masks Death will don—famine, disease, pollution, riots, and war—if we default to him the task of restoring the balance between mortality and natality.

And let us not commit the common mistake of perceiving the population explosion as exclusively a foreign phenomenon. America, too, has a serious population problem.

In 1950, there were 151 million people living in this country. In 1970, there are 204 million. By the year 2000—thirty years from now—that number will swell to 300 million. In short, the population of the United States will have doubled in the last half of the twentieth century.

What will the addition of 100 million people over the next

three decades mean to us as individual Americans? David Lilienthal, the former chairman of the Tennessee Valley Authority and the Atomic Energy Commission, provided part of the answer:

An additional one hundred million people will undermine our most cherished traditions, erode our public services and impose a rate of taxation that will make current taxes seem tame. . . . [Eventually] there comes a point at which a change in quantity becomes a change in quality—when we can no longer speak of "more of the same." And another one hundred million people will, I fear, make just that change in the joy of life in America.

In addition, our already critical environmental and pollution problems will be exacerbated; slums will spread; the crime rate will rise; our parks and beaches will grow even more crowded. And where shall we put 40 million more automobiles? Ponder that as you inch your way home tonight on a commuter-clogged freeway.

Those who argue there is no cause for alarm point to a steadily declining population growth rate in this country, which has fallen to nearly 1 per cent a year. However, even if we were to maintain this rate—and many demographers predict a rising rate as the 1946–47 crop of postwar babies begin to form families—the population of the United States will double every seventy years. In the short space of one hundred years, this would boost the number of people living in this country to 600 million—more than the present population of India.

This is the problem of aggregate population growth in America. There is also a structural or family problem.

Surveys have revealed, popular wisdom to the contrary, that low-income families in the United States desire *fewer* children than their middle- and upper-class counterparts. But they end up with larger families. Chicago's poor, for example, are saddled with a birth rate which equals that of India. The reason: over 4 million low-income women who want and would use family planning services and contraceptives are not receiving them.

And the price these women pay is not merely the inconvenience of more children than they desire. The price is increasingly long odds that they and their families will never escape from the poverty that oppresses them. For family size is a cause of poverty as well as an effect.

The dilemma facing the impoverished family is much like that confronting a developing nation. As the National Advisory Commission on Rural Poverty explained it:

A vicious circle of poverty and fertility is at work. . . . Because they [the poor] do not limit the size of their families, the expense of raising unwanted children on inadequate incomes drives them deeper into poverty. The results are families without hope and children without futures.

In other words, any effective campaign to eliminate poverty in this country must include programs which make family planning information and contraceptive devices available on a voluntary basis to all who desire them. For the right to be able to plan one's family is as essential a part of full freedom of opportunity as the right to a decent home, the right to an education fully commensurate with ability, and the right to a good job.

The history of life on this planet has been that of the unceasing struggle to adapt and survive. On its geological pages can be found the fossilized remnants of life forms that failed the evolutionary tests of competition and environment, life forms that committed their bodies to experimental adaptations in a blind genetic gamble for survival and lost.

Man alone among earth's children has escaped this evolutionary roulette game in which the stakes are life and death. He alone has assured his survival against any threats or demands nature may make. For with his brain and his hand, he has acquired the unique power to act upon nature itself. In effect, machines do man's evolving for him.

And herein lies the bitter irony of the twentieth century. For what nature has been unable to fashion, man has created. Using the very tools that have rendered us impervious to the forces of nature, we have invented the means of our own destruction. I am speaking of two bombs—the atom bomb and the population bomb.

What these bombs have in common, of course, is the capacity to terminate human history. However, they also exhibit crucial differences.

Nuclear weapons are storehouses of fantastic amounts of potential energy. But man must act before that energy becomes kinetic and, thus, destructive. In the absence of any human activity, these nuclear bombs continue to hang above the head of mankind like the sword of Damocles, but they will not fall. We have even fashioned a rude "balance of terror" which provides strong incentives for continued inaction.

The population bomb, on the other hand, is more accurately likened to a time bomb. It is in the process of going off and in time will explode with the same cataclysmic consequences as a nuclear holocaust—all without any conscious action on the part of men. Indeed, it is only through intelligent, co-ordinated action on a massive scale that we can avert disaster. For no balance exists to check the detonation of this bomb in the absence of human activity.

So in this sense the population bomb confronts us with a more likely threat to our survival than do our nuclear weapons. For governments are generally better organized to do nothing rather than something.

Are we then doomed by this time bomb of our own creation? It is a question only you and I can answer by our action or inaction in the next few years.

2

Revolutions of Despair

THE POPULATION problem, no matter how you approach it, is essentially a numbers game. If the birth rate exceeds the death rate, a population grows. Yet unless these numbers are translated into human terms at some point, the terrible urgency of the problem is difficult to comprehend. It was not until December, 1967, when I traveled through much of Latin America, that I finally experienced the human dimension of the population explosion.

International development has long been a concern of mine. With many others in the hemisphere, I had shared the hope that the Alliance for Progress, John F. Kennedy's bold aid experiment, would provide a model for economic and social development throughout the Third World.

To be sure, the Alliance has produced some notable successes since its inception in 1961. Tax reform has resulted in markedly increased revenues for most of the nineteen participating Latin American governments. Hygienic water systems serving over 10 million people have been constructed. Thousands of classrooms have been built and school enrollment has risen sharply.

However, on the eve of my trip, it was already evident that

the over-all performance of the Alliance had been a bitter disappointment even to its ardent supporters. Since the signing of the Alliance charter at Punta del Este, Uruguay, the standard of living of most Latin Americans had improved little, and in some parts of the continent, the quality of life had actually declined.

I wanted to observe first hand why the Alliance was not working. I wanted to see for myself what had gone wrong.

Much of what I discovered on that trip did not surprise me. In many places, progress has been blocked by the wealthy oligarchies and military cliques that dominate numerous Latin nations and which have refused to relinquish any of their power and privileges for the increased well-being of their peoples. In other instances, U.S. unwillingness to make available the resources these nations needed to build a sound infrastructure was at fault.

What did surprise me was the disconcerting realization that even with progressive, concerned Latin governments and American aid in sufficient quantity and kind, the Alliance still would have failed. The great destroyer of progress was population, population expanding so rapidly that it required heroic efforts to produce enough agricultural and industrial growth just to keep up.

It is difficult to convey the horror and despair one experiences wandering through the slums of the great Latin American cities. I sought to capture some of these feelings in a diary I kept at the time. Here is a brief excerpt:

I have been in Latin America only a few days and already I can see the catastrophic effects our medical assistance is having on this population. It's obvious everywhere that the rural populace has reaped the benefits of our disease eradication schemes and now the result is an exploding population critically straining the food supply. Everywhere I see that the rural agrarian populace is flocking to the panacea of relief in the cities—which are totally ill-equipped to deal with rural migrants. The poor live in slums in total abject despair and poverty.

Today I saw a horrible example of what the imbalance in the birth/death equilibrium has done to many of these people. I observed small children covered with open sores, the result of a protein deficiency known as "kwashiorkor." I saw children competing with black crabs for garbage. The whole thing is just like a nightmare or an 18th century novel written by some world traveler. I was told that in South America five out of every 10 children under 14 are severely retarded mentally or physically due to malnutrition. It's a matter of not enough food for the countless millions of unfortunate children.

I asked Peace Corps workers and AID officials about these things. I asked them if the large families were desired by the poor people of South America. They said, "No!" And they gave me an unforgettable example of just how desperate the poor people of South America are to limit and space their families. I was told that one of the major causes of death among women of child-bearing age was infection, resulting from self-induced abortions. The pitiful method used by these women is a wooden stick or a bent coat hanger. Pretty grim. Half the hospital spaces in Brazil are used by poor mothers either dying or dangerously ill because of their inept efforts to avoid another unwanted child. A sad commentary to our ability to advise and assist the underdeveloped countries in accordance with their most earnest needs.

Population growth in Latin America has created a paradoxical situation much like the one in *Alice In Wonderland* in which Alice is informed she must run faster to stay in the same place. In Peru, the population doubles every twenty-three years; the doubling time in Brazil is twenty-two years; in El Salvador, nineteen years. To make matters worse, more than 40 per cent of the population of the developing nations is under fifteen years of age and, therefore, unproductive.

Nations such as these must continually boost their rates of over-all economic growth just to maintain the low quality of life of their peoples. The burgeoning number of new mouths to feed each year makes per-capita gains in the standard of living and capital accumulation virtually impossible. In short, because it has a population that doubles every two decades, Latin America is not developing.

Nor are most of the nations of Asia and Africa for the same reasons.

It has become a cliché of modern history to state that revolutions occur when things are getting better, not worse; when the suppressed and impoverished realize that improvement is possible and grow impatient when their rising expectations are not quickly enough fulfilled.

However, if the next three decades produce the mass famines and falling living standards predicted for the developing nations, I believe we shall witness the emergence of a new genus of revolution—revolutions of despair. Lacking ideology and discipline, these revolutions will be spontaneous eruptions of desperation and hopelessness acted out by millions of men and women driven to the brink of starvation, legions of walking cadavers who have lost all faith in the ability of the existing order to produce progress and who are obsessed with a single objective—survival.

The fragile nation-states of Africa, Asia, and Latin America will surely be shattered by the force of this onslaught. And much of the world will almost certainly be plunged into a Dark Age of violence, chaos, and misery unequaled in human history.

What will all of the starvation and violence mean to America? As Dr. Paul Ehrlich has correctly observed:

We're unlikely . . . to get off with just our appetites spoiled and our consciences disturbed. We are going to be sitting on top of the only food surpluses available for distribution, and those surpluses will not be large. In addition, it is not unreasonable to expect our level of affluence to continue to increase over the next few years as the situation in the rest of the world grows ever more desperate. Can we guess what effect this growing disparity will have on our "shipmates" in the UDC's [underdeveloped countries]? Will they starve gracefully, without rocking the boat? Or will they attempt to overwhelm us in order to get what they consider to be their fair share?

This is a rhetorical question. I think we all know what the answer is.

Isolationist or internationalist? The population explosion has robbed us of that choice. Whether we like it or not, our destiny is inextricably bound to that of men in other nations. The bonds: the possibilities of "global ecological catastrophe, of global pestilence, and of global thermonuclear war."

What does the future hold for us? It all comes back to numbers, to man's ability to bring the birth rate back into balance with the death rate before we pass the point of no return.

PART II

Domestic and International Population Growth

3

U.S.: Preserving the Quality of Life

AT THE TIME of George Washington's first inauguration the population of the United States was less than 4 million people, only slightly greater than that of the state of Maryland today. During the early years of the Republic our population was growing at a rate of approximately 3 per cent a year, and the rate of increase remained at this level until 1860. From 1860 until around 1930 to 1940, the rate of increase in the population diminished until it reached a low point of .7 per cent a year.

Between 1790 and 1820 most of the increase in population reflected the difference between the number of births and the number of deaths. After 1820, and especially in the decades before and during World War I, immigrants from Europe made the major contribution to the growth of our population. Only about half of today's population consists of descendants of people living in this country during the early days of the Republic.

Birth and death rates in the United States until the early 1930's were closely related to the birth and death rates in the western and central European countries during the industrial revolution, the difference being, of course, the time in history these birth and death rates were reported and the influencing factors such as medicine, agriculture, and of course the industrialization of the developed countries in Europe. The economy of the United States, like the economies of many of the Western European countries, changed from predominantly rural and agricultural to largely urban and industrial during the late decades of the nineteenth and early decades of the twentieth centuries.

In the middle of the nineteenth century, voluntary family planning began to play an important part in the decline in fertility in the United States. By the time of the Depression in the 1930's, the spread of family planning programs had reached the point where women were bearing an average of only two children. The "voluntary" decrease in the birth rate was related to a number of factors, including changes in the basic economic environment, economic hardships of the Depression, and changing attitudes toward the family and its place in the rapidly developing society. Further, it was largely due to the rapid industrialization and the changing attitudes toward the economics of our family system. Interestingly enough, if the average of two children born in an American family had continued from the Depression days until the present time, the population of the United States would long ago have ceased to increase.

Mortality rates in early America were about 25 to 30 deaths per thousand annually, and the expectation of life at birth was less than forty years. By 1850 the expectation of life at birth had increased to forty-two years. In 1900 life expectancy rose to forty-seven years, and today it is slightly over seventy years.

In 1800 the annual birth rate in the United States was about 55 per thousand population. The rate fell steadily through the nineteenth century, and by 1900 it was below 30 per thousand. In the 1930's it was down to 20 per thousand. Then in the 1940's and 1950's the birth rate surged upward. One reason for the increase in the birth rate was an apparent change in attitude among prosperous, better-educated couples within certain elements of our society; they wanted to have larger families. Another principal reason was non-practice of birth control by the underprivileged and less educated Americans, who perhaps would have preferred smaller families. However, unfortunately, they had little knowledge of birth control practices, and access to information or contraceptive services was a thing of the future.

Generally speaking, American couples have tended to plan their families according to the trend of the times. Particularly, though, birth rates and large families among the poor or underprivileged are a cause for concern because of the impossible problems imposed on families who are already in a poverty class.

The population estimate of the United States for January, 1970, is approximately 204 million; population is increasing at the rate of a little over 1 per cent annually. The Census Bureau believes that the years 1965 through 1970 will mark the lowest period in the country's population history in terms of the annual rate of increase. Beginning in 1970 and continuing through 1990, the Census Bureau predicts that the annual growth rate will increase slightly, rising to 1.4 per cent per year. Experts estimate that the population could reach at least 336 million people by the year 2000 if the predicted rise in annual growth rates becomes a reality. This would be a net increase of approximately 132 million people in the next thirty-two years.

Compared to the tremendous population increases expected in the undeveloped countries of the world, the anticipated increase in population of 132 million in the United States may not be impressive. But what does it mean for us in the years ahead? Are we going to blunder into the twenty-first century sharing a scarcity of goods, services, advantages, and opportunities, so that each person in our swollen population will have less? Or will we begin to plan and act now to provide an adequate America for a new and expanding generation? Obviously, we must do what is necessary to assure not only adequate but improved nutrition, housing, clothing, education, health, and transportation in a non-polluted, beneficial, quality environment. All this will require greater, more responsible participation by the people of America if we are to move ahead, or even hold our own.

Looking one, two, and more generations into the future, it is the very quality of life that must be the concern of every citizen. The National Academy of Sciences–National Research Council, in its report "The Growth of U.S. Population," published in 1965 by the Council's Committee on Population, states, "In the very long run continued growth in the U.S. population will first be intolerable and then physically impossible." The committee warns that "rapid population growth will create difficulties in reaching America's noble goals of optimum education of all, universal abundance, and enriched leisure, equal opportunity, equality, beauty and creativity."

Population is an integral part of our total environment, and we are in danger of creating an environment too crowded for man to live on the planet earth! Of this hazard, the American Association for the Advancement of Science has said that man has been "using his power to alter his environment—with a blind pursuit of immediate objectives and a disregard of secondary effects that could endanger the very existence of life on this planet." The Association also stated:

Our institution of synthetic invasions of the natural web of life adds up to an appalling list of governmental and private errors that may result in environmental contamination that could have catastrophic effects on all of us. Commonly this discussion revolves around mistakes that could be made in judging the holes which nuclear explosions in the stratosphere would tear in the Van Allen radiation belt surrounding the earth, and the unanticipated environmental contamination produced by indiscriminate use of pesticides.

A common omission in such discussions of environment is population overcrowding. Sir Julian Huxley once wrote, "If we do not act soon man will become the cancer of the planet, destroying its resources, and eventually his own future self." Population is *the* issue in the existence of life on this planet, and man's ability to live within the altered environment that man himself has created. No longer can we think in terms of a large quantity of available natural resources for industrial use and vast expanses of land for cultivation. A casual look at our international trade statistics reveals that we are already an importer of natural resources by a significant amount, and our overseas dependence increases every year. Even the boundless resources of our hemisphere have a limit. Hence, any long-term population policy of the United States must also consider the same problems world-wide.

In an affluent society such as ours, it is easy to understand why the average American who lives in the suburbs or in the modern, efficient, high-rise urban areas looks only to the material benefits which the economic progress of America provides. However, material gains must now be thought of in terms of safeguarding and improving the total environment. This becomes especially important in view of innumerable problems of air and water pollution, the preservation of natural resources, and the achievement of livability, not to mention architectural style and beauty, in our urban environment.

Previously I have discussed population growth in the world according to international policy considerations and historical implications. All these factors are not intended to generate answers. It is essential to encourage a wider and deeper dialogue among the American people about what our social purposes should be and what is necessary to break the moral, political, and economic barriers to a better life for everyone. Before we can decide what should be the quality of our environment and what is necessary for the welfare of society, we need first to understand the implications of a population explosion at home and abroad. Dr. S. Dillon Ripley, secretary of the Smithsonian Institution, eloquently stated the importance of understanding this problem to the 90th Congress Joint House-Senate Colloquium on environmental quality:[1]

The most frightening aspect of Man's cultural development has been the establishment of conditions which permit the *fantastic population growth* we are witnessing today. No single development, excepting possibly the harnessing of nuclear energy, has raised such an ominous specter over the future of mankind as the present expansion of population. Unrestricted population growth out of phase with supporting natural resources not only compounds the problems of poverty and famine, the resolution of which provides mere existence; population size, combined with concentration, affects our ability to express the full range of our human potential. Crowding, herding, queues at every turn, noise, and ugliness are caging us and preventing us from finding the quality of life that we are striving for.

We know that the level of population resulting from the extrapolation of our present and even more conservative rates of growth simply cannot happen. We further know that even the 40-year [doubling rates] prediction cannot be tolerated. It is a fact that population size will ultimately be controlled by factors such as violence, famine, pestilence, or intelligent action. The first three, of course, exercise control in favor of existence. Only the latter course permits control in favor of fulfillment of the species.

But merely acknowledging the validity of Dr. Ripley's statement is not enough. All Americans must participate in this discussion. It has been our America up until now, it is ours in the foreseeable future. It is also up to us individually and collectively to stand up and be heard.

In the short run, population increases can produce, and

[1] U.S., Congress, Senate, Committee on Interior and Insular Affairs, and House, Committee on Science and Astronautics, Joint House-Senate Colloquium, *National Policy for the Environment: Hearing,* 90th Cong., 2d sess., 1968, pp. 211–12.

have produced, acute social, educational, and economic problems. Our schools and colleges are already being subjected to severe strains because of greatly increased numbers of students. Many American families today worry about placing a son or daughter in a college of their choice. When I attended school everyone who wanted to go to school, who had the money or the ambition and drive to work one's way through college, could go without any delay. Now, even for highly qualified students often there is a waiting period and too often, they go elsewhere. This is an unacceptable situation in a country which prides itself on its affluence and its ability to provide educational opportunity for all. Despite the vitality of our economy, practically 3 million U.S. citizens still cannot find work. The unemployment problem is compounded by automation, and by the increasing number of young people entering the labor force (almost 50 per cent of the American population is under the age of twenty-five).

The postwar population boom aggravated urban problems, increased the delinquency rate, and added to transportation problems. Our growing population threatens virtually to saturate all outdoor recreation areas within several hundred miles of any urban city, deplete our *non-renewable* natural resources, and severely reduce our available *living* space. The future quality of our living standards and the hallmark objectives of this country—life, liberty, and the pursuit of happiness—are threatened by the all-pervading effects of continued high rates of population growth.

Too many Americans believe a continued indefinite increase in population is somehow good. We should ask ourselves whether man, in nature, is subject to the same laws that govern other living things, particularly the law which says that for every species in a particular environment there is an optimum population. Man, who can rationalize and has thus far been able to alter his environment and alter his living to accommodate himself in that environment, must be also able to change his attitude toward population growth.

Benjamin Franklin once said, "They that can give up essential liberty to obtain a little temporary safety deserve neither liberty nor safety." This statement is usually associated with political liberty and patriotism. I believe it also has application to our continued quest to maintain our individual human dignity. We have long been engaged in a process of sacrificing essential liberty, the effects of which have yet to be felt. We have the knowledge and understanding to change attitudes on population problems. Not doing so in order to obtain a little security through increased material well-being jeopardizes maintenance of our essential liberty.

Perhaps we sacrifice a species of wildlife (the extinction of the passenger pigeon is an example), perhaps we strip a piece of land of its natural minerals (or cover as in strip mining), or perhaps we darken the sky with soot and smoke. We have done these things for material gains and not to preserve our individual liberty, our human dignity. The future quality of our life depends a great deal on the future psychological constitution of modern man. Are we capable of using our technological know-how for purposes other than material gain? Have we looked ahead in the direction we are moving? Have we really examined the facts of an age of revolution, an age of serious famine in the developing countries within the next five or ten years, an age of man who threatens to deprive himself of a future by refusing to recognize his predicament?

Today all Americans have a choice. Tomorrow I cannot answer for. Each American can remain a statistic, one of the billions in the world, or each American and other members of the community of man can take the responsibility to act, to influence the direction of humanity. The delicate environmental balance of an astronaut in a space capsule is similar to the delicate balance of man living on the spaceship earth. The size is different, the concept is the same. We are a part of the world we have made, and it is our responsibility to maintain the delicate balance between man and his environment.

4

Asia: Preserving Life

IN THE DEVELOPED, industrialized countries, including Japan and most of the European nations, at the present rate of growth, the population will double in fifty to one hundred years. In the United States and the Soviet Union, the population will double in about seventy years. However, two thirds of the people in the world live in the less developed countries in Asia (except Japan and parts of the Soviet Union), the Southwestern Pacific islands (principally the Philippines and Indonesia), Africa, the Caribbean islands, and Latin America (except Argentina and Uruguay). The annual rate of growth in these areas, if it continues at the present level of 2 to 3.5 per cent, will double the population in about thirty-five years. In these regions, where economic and social progress has been agonizingly slow and political unheaval a cause for international concern, the tremendously high rate of population growth could be disastrous for the whole world.

Asia is a region of extremes, covering an area of 16.5 million square miles, more than North and South America combined, it has the highest and lowest elevations in the world, from Mount Everest to the Dead Sea, extremes in climate, and an abundance of natural resources largely unexploited and in most cases unexplored. It was the cradle of the oldest cultures and the birthplace of the great religions. With more than half of the world's population, all but 15 per cent of the total available arable land has been brought under cultivation. Much of the land is either too arid or cold or mountainous for successful human settlement and agricultural development. Although millions of acres of land are available, most of the population is concentrated in the fertile plains and delta areas, where although poverty is a major problem, food crops are relatively plentiful and living conditions are tolerable.

Asia has great problems, including achieving political and economic stability, establishing free and representative governments, and moving into the modern industrialized world. But the continent's most challenging and basic problem is that of finding the means to support adequately its millions of people while reducing the rate of population growth. As we have seen, the tremendous increase in the world's population is due in large measure to man's increasing control over disease and death. In Asia this is also true. Though the death rate in Asia is still considerably higher than in the developed countries of the world, it is declining and is the principal factor in the increasing population. At the same time, the average birth rate has been maintained. As a result of the sustained high birth rate and the declining death rate, the population has grown so much that Asia has become deficient in grains and other food supplies, whereas before 1940 it was a surplus food-producing region.

The present Asian population of 1.6 billion people is expected to grow to over 3 billion by around the turn of the century. If this should really happen, Asia will have to more than triple the amount of food produced annually in order to feed its people adequately in the year 2000. Despite improved agricultural techniques, the prospects for this are extremely poor, in view of the dwindling supply of suitable land and the limited amount of capital available for agricultural programs.

If Asia should not be able to feed this anticipated population, will the United States be able to? I doubt it, for the same situation will exist in Africa and Latin America, too. Even if the most optimistic agricultural production estimates are realized, the United States cannot feed all the hungry billions in the world. The task of feeding the growing populations of India, China, Vietnam, Indonesia, and other Asian nations poses special and continuing problems. The Asian nations are attempting to implement national population policies with varying degrees of success. Some of these countries I have visited, others have been of interest to me as a public official concerned about international peace and security.

A discussion of Asian population problems in broad general terms would not provide a true picture of this complex and troubled region of the world. Therefore I have selected specific countries to illustrate the Asian population enigma.

FREE WORLD COUNTRIES

Japan, seventh among nations in population, is one of the most densely populated areas in the world. By the 1920's and 1930's, the Japanese had already experienced trouble with problems of food supply and population growth. The government went so far as to appoint a commission to examine the food problem. The commission's report recommended a birth control program, but the government aspired to gain more land in order to ease the pressures of population. Then with the coming of the 1940's and war, the death rates rose and the birth rates dropped, temporarily delaying government action. Postwar American medical assistance to Japan helped to lower the death rates, and with the return of Japanese soldiers, the country experienced a baby boom. This eventually resulted in a 2 per cent annual population growth rate. The people became concerned, for no longer was there new land to move to and the population density, already high, showed promise of reaching a level that would threaten the economy. Postwar Japan had become a democratic society, and the people demanded action.

In 1940 the government had passed a national eugenics law, stating that it was for the purpose of protecting the quality of the race. This law actually provided very little in the way of opportunities for the people to receive contraceptive information or enable the people to obtain legal abortions. In response to the public's concern, laws were passed in 1948 and 1952 further liberalizing official opinion on contraception and abortion. The 1948 amendment to the national eugenics law enabled private physicians to perform abortions, and in 1952 an amendment provided an even broader interpretation of the use of abortion and contraception.

Despite government support of a birth control movement, the major reductions in birth rates in Japan came through abortions which were supported privately rather than as a result of government policy. The pre-eminent factor in the reduction of births in Japan was the determination—or better, the popular participation—of the Japanese people. The government's major role was to make abortions permissible. Even today, a massive contraception program has only very minor governmental assistance; it is largely supported by private contributions.

Because the Japanese people voluntarily and conscientiously slowed their country's population growth, their rapid economic growth has not been threatened. Presently they realize an economic growth rate of approximately 10 per cent per year and anticipate doubling their per-capita income in the next decade. This is not to say that population is no longer a problem in Japan, for it is. If the declining birth rate continues, there are signs that the aging labor force will result in a shortage of manpower. Thus, the Japanese are now in a different phase of demographic transition, requiring new approaches.

The Japanese story will be repeated in other areas of the

world at different stages of man's demographic development. When it will depends on economic development, social transformation, and rapid yet subtle changes in the attitude of the people. It is a story with tremendous implications for other nations that would reverse the vicious web of poverty, illiteracy, low productivity, and high birth rates.

Postwar Japan was heavily industrial and had a higher level of education than other Asian countries. In other Asian nations where these conditions have not been achieved, the crucial role in the implementation of birth control will eventually be the responsibility of more assertive governments rather than private initiative, as it was in Japan after World War II. Only when the educational level can be raised to the extent that the popular participation of the people of a given country can contribute significantly to the total effort will private initiative be a major factor in solving the population problems of other Asian nations. Although changes in Asia are occurring, they have not begun to reach the level of participation that the Japanese people demonstrated is necessary for a real decline in birth rates to take place.

South Korea is estimated to have a population slightly over 30 million people, with an annual rate of total population increase of 2.4 per cent. At the present rate the population will double to 60 million by 1998. Fortunately, the country is beginning to do something about curbing the population growth rate, and both the government and the private sector have been encouraging and requesting assistance from the U.S. government and international organizations.

A breakthrough was realized in 1962 when a special advisory committee to the Korean Minister for Health and Social Affairs proposed a national family planning program. The Supreme Council of Korea approved this proposal and proceeded to recommend repeal of an old law forbidding importation of contraceptives. Government funds were made available for the program, and a population control effort was included in the Koreans' first five-year economic development plan.

The Korean program has been marked by creative leadership, intensive evaluation, considerable research, and a high quality of organization, administration, and supervision. Most of the reports about the South Korean family planning programs are encouraging.

The South Korean people lack many of the assets of their Asian neighbors; there is not enough arable land to feed the people and a lack of natural resources for industry. Despite this, their nature—competitive, proud, industrious—suggests that the future, if the international political scene does not affect South Korea adversely, is bright indeed. Increasingly, as income wages rise and aspirations for a higher standard of living go up, it will be essential that their family planning program continue along its successful route.

Off the coast of mainland China lies the island of Taiwan (Formosa), with a population of approximately 13 million and a density of 980 persons per square mile. It represents another example of an Asian country encountering the problems of limited amounts of land available for a fast-growing population. Aided by migration from mainland China, the population of Taiwan has doubled in the last twenty years and presently has an annual rate of growth of approximately 2.8 per cent.

Though the Chinese Nationalist government has thus far failed to establish a strong population policy, private organizations and international assistance have laid the groundwork for effective family planning in Taiwan. The traditional Chinese system of census taking, the reliable statistical information available from censuses taken in the past, and the maternal and infant care clinics that are in evidence throughout the country have provided the basic framework to conduct an ongoing population and family planning program.

A drop in population growth can be observed; in the mid-

1950's the population growth rate was approximately 3.8 per cent, and from that time on it steadily dropped to the present rate of 2.7–2.8 per cent annually. However, there are problems to be resolved. Over the past several decades continued high fertility in Taiwan has resulted in a very young population; approximately 44 per cent are less than twenty years of age. This places a tremendous burden on the productive capacity of the adult population. In the face of it, the private sector has mounted an impressive agricultural development program, helping people to buy time until the natural rate of increase of the population can be slowed.

Taiwan is an example of one of the few Asian nations who have succeeded in achieving real economic growth. As of 1965, U.S. foreign aid was virtually terminated. The Joint Commission on Rural Reconstruction (JCRR) is now classified as a model for other nations who would aspire to develop a comprehensive community reconstruction program.

Perhaps nowhere else in Asia is the population problem so acute as in Indonesia. This country has the sixth largest population in the world with approximately 115 million people. Two thirds of them live on the island of Java, with an average population density of 1,425 per square mile. The annual rate of increase is between 2.3 and 2.7 per cent or about 2.5 million people a year. In addition to the population problem (or perhaps because of it), Indonesia has for many years been plagued by political and social unrest and an unstable economy.

Because of severe inflationary factors, stabilizing the economy has been accorded the highest priority since 1966. Based upon the present estimate of a 2.3 per cent population growth rate, Indonesia will require an economic growth rate of 2.5 per cent, food production increases will have to reach a minimum of 4 per cent, and an investment rate of 15 per cent of the national income must be achieved. Thus it appears that the economic progress of Indonesia is inseparable from her ability to cope with population problems.

Medical care and assistance to Indonesia from the Western world has substantially reduced the mortality rate, with no comparable lowering of the birth rate. This has resulted in a greater number of Indonesians entering the potential work force annually. The lack of available jobs for these young adults and inadequate training for those positions that need to be filled create an atmosphere of frustration and foster social and political unrest.

The Indonesian government has only recently realized the necessity for establishing a national population and family planning program. On February 8, 1968, the president of Indonesia finally approved the establishment of a quasi-governmental ad hoc committee to assist in organizing a national family planning program. Shortly after this, the president approved a modest budget and asked the National Planning Organization, the Institute of Demography, and the Indonesian Planned Parenthood Association to prepare a document outlining a modest family planning program for the country's five-year economic development plan.

There are other encouraging indications of the government's attitude toward population. The president has supported family planning publicly on at least one occasion recently, and there is close cooperation between the Ministry of Health and voluntary associations on this issue. Also, the existing network of maternal and child health centers will undoubtedly provide the basis for the development of a national family planning program.

There are shortcomings to the government's approach; however, with so many acute economic problems, it is unlikely that a national family planning program will be assigned high priority. Since Indonesia has an agriculturally based economy, the government believes that by concentrating on agriculture (improved grains, more effective use of fertilizers, better farm equipment, etc.), it can keep up with the population's many and growing needs. It will not be able to do so, however, unless the population growth is slowed. The emphasis on short-term, five-year planning programs will be a hindrance to government officials in allocating funds and resources for a long-term family planning program.

One recent attempt to reduce the tremendous overcrowding on Java by transferring people to less densely populated islands has been unsuccessful. The government will have to find another solution. The key element in the future prospects for slowing Indonesia's population growth lies in the government's willingness to give family planning a priority equal to that of agricultural development.

Thailand is an Asian country that has enjoyed a relatively high rate of economic growth. With an agriculturally based economy, Thailand as recently as 1965 reached a peak of rice export volume. So why include Thailand in a discussion of population problems in Asia? Because, despite all evidences of sustained economic growth, there is just around the corner a population squeeze which threatens their economic growth.

In the past few years there has been unmistakable evidence that something must be done in addition to improving agricultural production if the nation is to continue along its upward-bound economic road. Rice surpluses, long the backbone of government revenue sources, have shown a perceptible decline recently. At the same time, the level of rice exportation has continued undiminished, causing a decline in domestic surpluses. This has not presented the Thai government with an immediate problem, but the trend is unmistakable. Domestic rice surpluses serve to bolster that portion of the urban-industrial sector (poverty-level group) which relies on the government to subsidize them.

Producing more rice, diversifying the economy to cope with a decline in exports, and encouraging non-rice agriculture production will help the squeeze. However, it will not be of much help if long-range, government-supported initiatives are not undertaken to slow the high population growth rate.

The history of Thailand's birth control program shows that until recently the government did not view population growth as a necessary ingredient to economic growth. Then in 1959 a World Bank report stated that Thailand's birth rate was too high and recommended that the government begin to encourage birth control programs. However, in the past ten years, despite strong recommendations from several planning groups (the latest a particularly strong proposal emanating from a locally held population seminar in 1968), the Cabinet has been reluctant to establish a strong population policy along with other national priorities.

It was not until 1967 that the Cabinet approved a report recommending that the National Development Board be responsible for developing a national population policy. This was done and now provides the basis for the current Thai effort in this field.

Many important undertakings have had inauspicious beginnings. The Thai family planning program is no exception. In 1965 the Thailand family planning program began very humbly, from a hospital-based family health clinic which began by providing family planning services and advice only one afternoon each week. In a mere eight months the program had grown to such proportions that more than eight thousand women had been provided with IUD's and an additional fifteen hundred women were on a waiting list. The tremendous increase in volume of services was accomplished with virtually no publicity, showing how receptive the Thai women were to the idea of limiting and planning their family once they were given access to information and services.

Senator Edward Kennedy and I were privileged to visit Thailand in 1965. While there I visited the Chulalongkorn Hospital Family Health Clinic referred to above. Under the able direction and supervision of Dr. M. L. Kashetra Sindoongs, this hospital provided what could be the basis of a rapidly expanding Thai government commitment to support a national family planning program. Typical of many "de-veloping-country" leaders was the stated reason for an important Thai Cabinet leader's opposition to the program. He stated essentially that Thailand could not become a "powerful nation" until the population was at least 50 million.

The current estimate of Thailand's population, based upon a 1960 census, ranges from 33 to 35 million. If the current estimated rate of growth (3.2 per cent) continues, the 1960 population (26.3 million) will have doubled by 1980.

As in other countries, the positive effects of slowing present rates of population growth in Thailand will not be observed immediately. It takes from twenty to thirty years before the over-all economic factors can be measured and compared with previous years. Generally, the negative effects of sus-tained population growth would not be felt for some time; when that time came the resource commitment would be substantially higher, and in that period of inaction adverse economic and social trends would inevitably set in. We can look at this in a historical perspective and see that population trends are economic indicators. And in this era of population revolutions our response must be dynamic—a human response to a human problem. Science and technology will provide the tools, the people must provide the proper attitudinal response. With notable exceptions in the Cabinet the Thailand govern-ment has not officially opposed population and family pro-grams in their country. Yet there is still some reluctance to reverse the attitude of the past that somehow more people meant economic prosperity. The people are ahead of the government and willing to plan their families responsibly. We should require at least the same in our foreign aid policy, that is, that the government follow the popular interest of the people. Let us encourage policy that would not deter their bright future.

India ranks second in population size in the world and seventh in land area. It covers an area of 1.2 million square miles, with a population estimated at anywhere from 500 million to 580 million people. They are distributed over 17 states, 11 union territories (comparable to the District of Columbia), 326 administrative districts, some 2,690 towns and cities, and 564,258 villages. India claims about 14 to 15 per cent of the world's population and 2.4 per cent of the world's land area. A good comparison of the population density of India is to relate it to the size of continental United States. Although India is only approximately two fifths the size of the United States, she has about two and one-half times our population. The estimates of birth and death rates may be underestimated or overestimated, the former being more likely. What we do know is that the population is increasing at the rate of approximately 2.5 per cent per year, which if not checked will double the population to an incredible 1 billion in less than thirty years. Estimates are that a baby is born every second and a half, or about 21 million births a year. There are about 8 million persons dying annually in India. Subtracting this figure from the estimated number of births leaves 13 million people annually being added to the present population. This would be equivalent to Australia's entire population.

One area of the economy showing relative progress is agricultural production. Since 1947, when India achieved political independence, agricultural production has continued to improve far beyond any comparable period prior to 1947. But political freedom without substantial economic advancement and social progress is largely meaningless and creates frustration and a dangerous political climate. For this reason India has embarked upon a series of planned economic development programs. These have been largely unsuccessful due to several factors; principal among them is a high population growth rate. Thus, although the availability of goods and services has greatly increased in the last ten years, the per capita consumption has shown no increase. In 1966 and 1967 weather and other natural conditions caused a severe decrease in the amount of food produced in India. Widespread starvation was staved off largely due to American wheat and rice exports. In 1968, the harvest resulted in a bumper crop of nearly 96.6 million tons compared to the bare minimum of 72 million tons in 1966. Despite the harvest of nearly 100 million tons food consumption per capita has not increased markedly. Why? Simply because the additional millions each year nullify most of the food production increases.

The burgeoning population is affecting virtually every aspect of Indian life. As I have mentioned before with regard to other Asian countries, the rate of growth severely limits the ability of the government to provide better educational and public health facilities and other basic public services. India's inability to improve its over-all standard of living is evidenced by the national income figures.

Total national income increased from 86 billion rupees during 1948 to 149 billion rupees in the period 1966–67, or an increase of 73 per cent over a period of nearly twenty years. During this same period of time per capita income increased a meager 19 per cent. This trend places India's per capita income among the lowest in the world. Viewed over the past twenty years, their rate of over-all national development has been virtually zero. India has not only remained economically stagnant but in many respects has reduced its position of economic well-being in relation to the rest of the world.

Recent developments indicate that science and technology have provided India a few years of bargaining time in which to sustain an all-out effort to reduce drastically the population growth rate. Also, the implementation of new policies within the Indian government promises to add considerably to their agricultural production capacity. The severe droughts of 1965 and 1966 caused considerable hardship and contributed in many respects to the rapid implementation of new agriculture policies in 1967.

The Indian government is attempting to solve its population problems primarily through the development of a viable birth control program in addition to modern agricultural improvement programs. There are other ways in which the Indians are attempting to solve their population problems, notably through large-scale heavy industrialization and the encouragement of internal migration to ease regional pressures. However, these will be of minor significance to the future economic prospects of India unless a sustained, imaginative family planning program can be mounted and maintained *for many years to come*. The population growth rate must be severely reduced. There is no other intelligent, humane answer to India's many problems.

The important element in any program—measuring success—in the case of India indicates that family planning has met with at best only marginal success. Approximately 2.4 per cent of the married couples in their reproductive years are using contraceptives. If India is to reduce substantially the growth rate, estimates are 65 per cent of the reproductive age couples must regularly use 100 per cent effective contraceptives. Based upon present population estimates and current level of activity, around *30 million reproductive-age women must be reached*, or an increase of 2000 to 3000 per cent in the level of activity of present family planning programs. Clearly unprecedented levels of technical and financial assistance will be needed from the developed countries. India cannot do it alone.

The government, under the leadership of Prime Minister Mrs. Indira Gandhi, Chairman of the Federal Cabinet Committee on Family Planning, decreed that family planning is the number-one priority alongside the improvement of agricultural production for the country. This is probably the single most important factor—the government's awareness that population growth is the nation's number-one problem—in looking at the Indian situation with any semblance of optimism.

The future success of a family planning program in India lies in motivating the people to accept family planning, a better contraceptive method, more money, and trained health manpower. Recent studies in India show that over 70 per cent of the mothers and fathers of all castes, religions, and income groups are in favor of or are practicing family planning. But this desire is not sufficient motivation to send them to a clinic to learn about a method of family planning and to use it rationally. What is necessary is to motivate the entire country, regardless of religion or caste, to want to control or to space and plan their families. Before this can be done the complex, many-state country of India must be studied in depth to understand the motivational problems and what will be necessary to carry out a successful national program. A very simple and easily understandable method of contraception is also needed. As one leading Indian official, Minister of Family Planning Dr. S. Chandrasekhar, recently stated: "Perhaps the most difficult problem before us is the choice of contraceptive that is acceptable under Indian conditions, particularly in the depressed rural areas where privacy, running water, electricity, and knowledge of reproductive physiology and, most important, motivation, are more or less absent." The present methods of controlling births available to India are sterilization, abortion, the IUD introduced in 1965, the pill, and the condom. Probably the most effective method thus far in India is sterilization. IUDs, the pill, and abortion have all suffered setbacks of one kind or another, and any statistics I read, if examined carefully, show that the widespread use of IUDs and the pill have not been successful. Perhaps the research now being done on the mini-pill, or the morning-after-pill, or the injectables will provide an effective, safe method acceptable to the Indians, one that would require a minimum amount of supervision and education.

Fundamentally, India, although it has raised the priority on population programs to the level necessary, has failed to implement the education and motivation aspects of the family planning program through existing institutions, i.e., schools, trade unions, private enterprise, etc. The present program is generally intended to impose a motivational educational structure on the whole country, a dubious procedure considering India's size.

The population problems which confront India now will be with the people for years to come, and only an outstanding and unprecedented assistance effort on the part of the developed countries of the world will avert famine and political and social chaos in India. Her present five-year economic plan indicates a need on her part to work through existing institutions. The United States should require that she do so in her financial assistance agreements.

COMMUNIST CHINA

One cannot discuss Asia without discussing the nation which makes up one fourth of the world's population, Communist China. There is admittedly a paucity of information concerning mainland China; however, an attempt at understanding China's population problems may provide a clue to their future and international political posture. Perhaps most important, an appreciation of the population problems facing the Chinese brings into sharp focus the implications of population growth as it relates to international peace and security.

The free world has had few substantive exchanges with China since Mao Tse-tung gained control of the country in 1949. Official U.S. reports have had important omissions, and generally all analysis is hedged with doubt. Moreover, the Chinese Communists themselves do not collect much data and do not release much of the data they have. There is therefore a scarcity of information about China *in* China.

Population data on Communist China end, for all practical purposes, with the end of 1957. Because of statistical inadequacies and limited time coverage, the official data usually have to be revised or adjusted and supplemented by estimates and projections, if the development of China's population is to be seen in perspective with sufficient accuracy to permit useful comparisons with that of the rest of the world. Also, and this is important, any assessments of China's population policies have to be considered in the context of the Chinese Communists' domestic policy as a whole.

The major source of information on China's population, and the basis for subsequent projections, is the census of June 30, 1953. Free-world scholars have carefully analyzed the data and have arrived at an informed "guesstimate" of 600 to 640 million people. This is based on the evaluation that the 1953 census omitted a large proportion of the population. After thorough analysis, the population total has been carefully projected to a level somewhere between a low estimate of 879 million and a high estimate of 1,123 million by 1968. Thus, in the extremely short space of thirty-three years, mainland China's population may very well have doubled in size. By 1986 it would total *four times* the anticipated population of the United States for that year.

The problems confronting China today are not altogether unlike those the Communists faced when they took over the country in 1949. Then more than 85 per cent of the population produced the food supply in an age-old system of peasant agriculture. The Communists, armed with Marxist ideology modified by Mao Tse-tung's doctrine, set about proving to the world that they could transform a traditional agricultural society into an industrial giant of the modern era. Twenty years later all evidence suggests that the great experiment has not proved successful.

Problem after problem has presented itself despite a strong social control system. One of the many flaws of Mao's great design seems to be his inability to perceive clearly the importance of having a population policy that relates to his plan for industrialization of the country. The Chinese Communists apparently have yet to comprehend fully the importance of a sound population policy, as evidenced by the government's fluctuations of position on this matter.

Whatever prestige China has had under the Communists

has been due to a relative national unity in the years prior to the present Cultural Revolution. When Chairman Mao and his colleagues took over the country in 1949, it was in a state of chaos. They brought it to a degree of internal order and discipline seldom witnessed in that land. They made the most of this for propaganda purposes, yet the achievement was real and substantial. Apparently, it is in the economic sphere and, particularly, in agriculture that they have had the least success, even from the earliest years of the regime. And it is in the political sphere, internally, that they apparently have had their most recent acute crises.

Estimates of population growth rates indicate that China has already added some 200 million people to her population since 1949. Unless one is willing to assume success in economic development and some striking new gains in reducing fertility, or both, it would be reasonable to estimate that at least 300 to 350 million more people may be added to China's population by at least the year 2000, if not before. It is questionable whether China could, in fact, support a population of more than a billion under the economic conditions likely to prevail by the year 2000. Whatever the indications or estimations, clearly the leaders of Communist China did not realize the shattering effect population growth rates would have on their various five-year economic growth plans.

The bane of all regimes throughout history that have tried to rule the people of China has essentially been that they have not given sufficient attention to the problem of how to feed the increasing millions of China. The Chinese Communists, however, have devoted much attention to this problem. Their great handicap has been that they tried to increase food production almost entirely by the socialization of agriculture during the 1950's. After the food crises of 1960–61, they finally recognized the need to give priorities, manpower, and capital to industries that supported agriculture, the chemical fertilizer and farm implement industries. They faced the food problem with every show of reluctance, but they *did* face it in the end—though not in connection with their fast-growing population.

To understand the appalling inconsistencies in China, it is important to realize the Chinese unwillingness to accept the fact that domestic population policies are essential to economic growth. Partly because they were so unwilling to recognize the urgency of their population problems, the Chinese Communists were unable to formulate and adhere to effective policies. They were hampered by the fact that they were Marxists, and Marxism in effect declares that there can be no population problems in a socialist country. However, during the period of the five-year plan, some Communist Chinese leaders did recognize the need for population policy in what were, for all practical purposes, not Marxian but rather neo-Malthusian terms. They got around their dilemma by saying that China's population problems were a heritage of the past and not, therefore, indigenous to socialism. Significantly, in 1957, when the population policies were fluctuating, they did say that planning population growth is essential to planning economic development in a socialist society. So in a sense, one must grant that, however unwillingly, they did for a time accept the fact that population policy was essential to economic growth. These fluctuations are highly significant for they reflect a fundamental ambivalence on the population question as the Chinese Communist leaders vacillated between doctrinaire Marxist hopes and cold Malthusian fears.

A recognized authority has documented the basic fluctuations of the Chinese Communists on population policy, and these are summarized by phases as follows:[1]

Phase I, 1949–1953

The Chinese denounced birth control as a method of reducing their numbers. They banned the importation of contra-

[1] *Population studies* XVI, No. 1 (1962), pp. 38–57, John Aird, "Population Policy in Mainland China."

ceptives and prohibited abortion. Marx in his ideological quarrel with Malthus described population theory as "a contrivance of capitalists to rationalize the depressed status of the working class." Marx concluded that, under socialism, unemployment would disappear and so would population problems. The Chinese initially accepted this theory and ignored population as an issue.

Phase II, August 1953–August 1956

Partly because of the surprisingly large census figure of 1953, the period from August 1953 to August 1956 was marked by indecision on the part of top Party leaders. Official reactions were inconsistent with Marxist ideology, and the general atmosphere at policy-making levels was apprehensive about the consequences of rapid population growth. In September, 1954, at the First National People's Congress, first session, Shao Li-tsu recommended that "propaganda on contraception be strengthened and limitations on techniques for birth control loosened." Apparently nothing happened after Shao's initial speech, for he submitted a motion at the second session in July, 1955. This motion was approved, but again nothing much happened until the important directive encouraging postponement of marriage and family limitation was issued by the Ministry of Health in August, 1956. There were indications that individuals not connected with the government or party were publicizing the arguments for birth control. It is significant that, although hardline Marxists in the Communist party and the government were known to be opposed to birth control and population policies designed to discourage high fertility, they were never allowed to answer Shao's arguments, either in speeches to the National People's Congress or in articles in the newspapers. This indicates great hesitancy on the part of the government, probably because of the government's original denouncement.

Phase III, September 1956

Chou En-lai confirmed official support of birth control at the Eighth National Party Congress, and a full-swing birth control program went into effect. About this time, Mao Tse-tung announced that a socialist society could afford a difference of views and called for an open debate on the major issues of the day. This was the Hundred Flowers period. After some reluctance, the "experts" (intellectuals) released a barrage of criticism on all fronts that rocked the Chinese Communist party. Scholars began to make plans to restore courses in such subjects as sociology and population, and they began to express a pessimistic view of the government's greatly advertised economic plans. One eminent scholar went so far as to suggest that control of excessive population increases was vital to the success of industrialization. Still another openly endorsed the Malthusian population theory. These scholars were saying, in effect, that without control of population growth, the future of socialism was in danger. These are examples of expressions and activities which so thoroughly upset the party leaders that the split between party and academia is still not repaired. Other issues, of course, besides population policy, split the party leaders. The controversies that had developed brought about a termination of the Hundred Flowers period and the start of the extremely repressive "great rectification" drive in June, 1957.

Phase IV

Shortly after the controversies of the Hundred Flowers period, the party leaders denounced the critics as "bourgeois rightists." For a while the birth control campaign continued; then, in 1958, the birth control program was suddenly dropped. Actually, after June, 1957, only one critic continued to attack the official line on birth control. He was Ma Yin-ch'u, rector of Peking University, an eminent Chinese scholar and personal friend of Chou En-lai. His friendship with Chou shielded him, not from vicious press criticism, which he got in great quantity, but from outright purging. By 1960, when the whole country was on the brink of famine, Ma's pessimistic views on population had been silenced, and he was dismissed from his university post. From this point on, until 1962, the party generally refused to admit the continuing problem of population growth as a deterrent to its economic programs.

Phase V

In 1957, at the close of the period of the first five-year economic plan, it became obvious to government officials that China's economic transition was faltering in spite of an accelerated program of socialization. In 1958 the party took hold of the statistical machinery of the country and inflated production figures while marking the next three years as the Great Leap Forward period. The government's design was to mount the necessary material resources to meet ever higher production goals. However, the resulting enthusiasm produced false hope instead of improving production. The complete socialization of what was left of private industry and the development of farm communes completely destroyed private incentive. Moreover, there was a series of natural disasters, such as drought, floods, and infestations of locusts. As a result, the entire country experienced near-starvation from 1959 through 1961.

It would appear that China had failed to learn from the experiences of the past that population problems should be a principal factor in economic planning. However, there was a reason for their apparent failure to understand. Government leaders received reports of bumper crops which they took to be the fruits of both theory and experience. It was on the strength of these fraudulent reports that attempts were made to refute so-called bourgeois opinions on the population growth rate problem. This period continued to represent failure of the Communists to resolve population and food production realities with Chinese Marxist philosophy which states that "labor is capital." All indications pointed to a continuing inability to resolve this dilemma.

Phase VI, May 1958–Fall of 1959

During the beginning of this phase, the leaders were supremely confident that China had at last rounded the corner on the food problem. However, before the end of 1958 there were signs of faltering in China's attempt to have an economic boom under the aegis of the Great Leap Forward program. There was a growing awareness that the miracles of production were fictitious and that the production figures had been fabricated at the request of the party. Morale collapsed, and the country entered a period during which the government was merely holding tight on questions concerning the country's ability to feed its population. No mention was made in public this time of the problems of the economic plans.

The end of this phase marked the collapse of the Great Leap Forward program. By the fall of 1959, confidence in an economic boom had definitely come to an end. Food shortages were again reported in various areas, casting doubt on the supposed bumper crops of the year before. From 1959 until about April, 1962, most of the illusions were dead or dying. The Chinese had come to a realization that there were real problems at hand.

Phase VII

In April, 1962, the Chinese Communists resumed their policy of promoting the postponement of marriage and family limitation. They continued this policy until June, 1966. Then, abruptly, public mention of birth control came to a definite halt.

Phase VIII, Fall of 1966–Present

During this phase, the first year of which embraced the Cultural Revolution, leaders denounced birth control as part of the "poisonous stuff of revisionism," spread by Liu Shao-ch'i, and young people began to violate the policies on delayed marriage by getting married in droves and starting their families early. There was widespread adverse reaction within the country against policies that had first been officially disclosed as Maoist policy. This phase seems to have ended about September or October, 1967, when it was officially disclosed that, contrary to what some people thought, birth control policy was a policy promoted by Mao Tse-tung, not Lui Shao-ch'i.

A study of all these changes and vacillations indicate that the Chinese Communists find themselves deeply split on political and economic policies. The changes in Chinese population policy seem to be attributable to and correlated with the government's frustrated attempts to achieve inflated economic goals.

The Cultural Revolution has in my opinion diminished China's image of power in world affairs. This opinion is based upon two factors. First, I think China's progress has been exaggerated in recent years, partly because of the ambivalance of the Chinese leaders on the population question and their inability to plan realistically for the country's economic development.

Second, China's capacity to engage in international relations and to back its claims of success and power with the veiled threat of force has declined because of China's internal political and economic difficulties. In the 1950's the Chinese enjoyed a favorable political environment in many parts of the world because their approaches to problems had yet to receive a critical test. Now that evaluation of their approaches to problems has revealed their inability to maintain internal stability, China's achievements and prospects seem much less spectacular than they did before June, 1966. In one respect China's international importance is certainly justified, for in the future this country, representing one-fourth of the world's population, is likely to affect the lives of all Asians to a degree yet to be determined.

A major lesson to be learned is that the relationship of population growth rates to plans for economic growth cannot be ignored, whether in a laissez-faire economy or a completely socialized one as in China. The Chinese leaders have been deeply concerned about the continuing food crisis; they just have not been able to marshal a consensus within their own party ranks on the course of action to pursue.

Today the purge known in China as the Great Proletarian Cultural Revolution is sweeping party ranks. This unprecedented purge and China's ideological split with Russia have deprived the country of foreign sources of investment credit, industrial plant equipment, and desperately needed technical assistance. This deprivation, combined with isolation from other outside economic resources, a rapidly growing population, confusion about population policies, and the elimination of incentives for industrial and agricultural production, provides all the right conditions for economic and political instability. The future of China's efforts to achieve economic, social, and political stability will be determined in large measure by the ability of new Chinese leadership to resolve internal differences between party leaders and economic planners.

From what I have been able to observe, Asian countries vary widely in terms of their readiness to move from an agricultural society to a modern industrial one. One reason is that readiness and will to develop an effective design in pursuit of economic growth differs considerably from nation to nation. A great deal depends on the people and the receptivity of the social structure to change. The nations in Asia, Africa, and Latin America all have one thing in common that contributes to the complexity of attitudes toward social change; each has its individual social and cultural heritage.

They all have their individual personalities requiring specific and distinct approaches to their national programs. Success in co-ordinating this motley set of attitudes will only come through the internationalization of attitudes—in this case attitudes concerning population and family planning. America can act to encourage that population planning assistance be approached regionally through the relevant Asian development programs. For example, this can be done through the Economic Commission for Asia and the Far East (ECAFE), the Asian Development Bank, the World Bank, and other similar international bodies. The world community must act and work like a world community if it is to realize mutually beneficial programs.

5

Africa: Preserving a New Frontier

THE NEW African nations provide unprecedented promise and opportunity for excellence in this era of human history. Nowhere else in the world is there a better laboratory of human behavior in which men can seek a better life for mankind. The possibilities are unlimited for economic growth, political and social stability, and a better quality of life for present and future African generations.

Africa's place of importance in world affairs has increased markedly in the last decade, and I believe it is important for us all to have an appreciation of the complexity of this great and troubled continent, its past and present problems, and its future prospects. In the world today and in the world of our children tomorrow, the economic, social, and political changes that take place in Africa will increasingly affect America and other nations.

With some 11,685,000 square miles, Africa is the second largest continent in the world. There are, however, estimated to be only 328 million people living there, or less than 10 per cent of the world's population. Despite the world's lowest population density (25 people per square mile compared to 157 per square mile in Europe and 110 in Asia), Africa has population problems that promise to create serious economic and social crises that threaten the continent's future development and place in world affairs.

Evaluations of the continent's economic progress fail to show any hope of a substantial break in the vicious cycle of poverty which encompasses most of Africa's people. Because the population is expanding at a faster rate than the economy, real economic gains are reduced although economic growth is occurring (an average annual growth in gross domestic product of 4.2 per cent between 1960 and 1964). Population increases have absorbed much of the gains in food production and housing, and social services have failed to keep pace with the rising demand. Governments must choose between increasing social expenditures and capital investment to spur economic growth. High birth rates cause the economically active portion of the population to support an increasing number of dependents. Even with increased productivity it is difficult, therefore, to realize any over-all rise in the standard of living. Furthermore, *population growth* has not been anticipated sufficiently and provided for in development planning. Economic analysts are becoming concerned that Africa's current development plans for its present population of 328 million will fall far short of creating an economic structure to provide for its population of an estimated 900 million by the end of the twentieth century. The African nations must recognize that population changes will have a major impact on development prospects. The United States and other developed nations can do no less than to stress this in their plans for assistance to African nations, and particularly in five spheres of development—public health, education, employment, housing, and agriculture—where population increases will place the greatest pressure on Africa's available resources.

Africa's battle for health is a complex one, particularly in relation to population pressure and development. One noted ecologist has observed that where penicillin is introduced, birth control must also be introduced in order not to upset the natural balance between man and his resources. Falling death rates and increasing (or sustained) birth rates can spell economic disaster, especially in areas where economic development cannot keep pace with the new demographic conditions. However, reduced infant mortality rates resulting from improved care of infants and their mothers can have a positive demographic impact by leading to reduced birth rates. Presently, African families have as many children as possible in order to assure the survival of a few. As fewer children die at birth and more children survive beyond the age of five, the African birth rate can perhaps be expected to be naturally slowed. However, at the current rate of population growth (2.3 per cent per year), birth control will remain a necessity if Africa's population is not to outdistance its economic resources during the coming decade.

Health, perhaps the greatest of all human needs, is Africa's greatest problem. The two out of three African children who, on the average, survive beyond the age of five begin a life-long battle for survival. Malnutrition is perhaps the greatest child-killer, for it causes about 12 or 13 per cent of the deaths of children in Africa. The horrible protein deficiency disease, kwashiorkor, which has gained world-wide attention because of the tragic situation in Biafra, is a disease common throughout Africa. Measles takes the life of an average of 15,000 children a year in Nigeria alone. In certain areas of Africa, up to 25 per cent of the children are afflicted with tuberculosis. By the time an African child reaches adulthood there is a good chance that he will be enfeebled by one of the many parasitic diseases rampant on the African continent. His productive capacity will be permanently reduced as he becomes chained to a lifetime of disease. A 1963 report estimated that as many as 75 per cent of the rural people of the United Arab Republic were suffering from bilharziasis, an infection spread by a type of snail commonly found in African waters. In general, little progress has been made against this disease throughout Africa, and it has actually increased in some areas where modernization programs have brought new irrigation facilities and thus created new breeding grounds for the durable bilharziasis parasite. New drugs, insecticides, and public health programs have made inroads against diseases; however, malaria, smallpox, measles, sleeping sickness, and tuberculosis are still major problems. In one area of Ethiopia, one person in ten is a leper. Malaria-carrying mosquitos and tsetse flies bearing sleeping sickness still infest large areas of fertile land and virtually cause it to be closed to cultivation because farmers fear contact with the infected insects.

To combat sickness in Africa, one of the first necessities is the creation of new attitudes toward health. Freedom from illness is so uncommon that poor health is an accepted fact of life. Faced with so many demands upon their resources, African governments generally give low priority to health programs in their economic plans. Though there has been a heartening trend toward the inclusion of national health programs in development plans, they generally receive an allotment of about 7 per cent or less of a national budget. Outside assistance is mandatory if African nations are to have sufficient resources for truly effective public health programs.

In recognition of this situation, U.S. Agency for International Development programs have placed a new emphasis on public health. During the 1969 fiscal year, U.S. AID teams hoped to inoculate 45 million people in nineteen West African and Central African countries against smallpox and measles. American foreign assistance programs, however, must also help African health officials combat attitudes and food taboos that reinforce malnutrition and inhibit effective health care. Rigorous self-help programs in the field of public health should be given every encouragement possible through a significant U.S. effort to provide comprehensive technical assistance while the Africans themselves become involved in the provision of services to the people.

While modernization and the development of public health programs create hopes for lifting the curtain of sickness, population factors raise new obstacles to better health care. For example, rapid urban growth places a strain on existing health facilities and creates a demand for health care greater than a city's capacity to construct and staff new health centers. Sanitation facilities are impossibly strained by the urban population squeeze, resulting in an increase in disease that intensifies the need for more health facilities. Yet city dwellers enjoy a greater opportunity for health care than the millions of rural Africans who live totally outside the world of modern medicine.

One of the greatest obstacles to creating additional health services is the shortage of trained medical personnel. A recent World Health Organization (WHO) report indicated that while some areas of the developed world enjoy a ratio of one doctor to 500 to 1,000 people, the *average* ratio in Africa, including foreign doctors and missionaries, is one doctor to 25,000 to 50,000 people. These statistics do not tell the whole story for many African nations. For example, in Ethiopia the ratio of doctors to potential patients is one to 68,500. (In the United States there is one doctor for every 680 people, a ratio that American public health experts consider dangerously low). The present facilities of Africa's medical schools, 90 per cent staffed by non-Africans, will be unable to turn out within the next ten years the estimated 18,000 graduates necessary to meet the goal of establishing a ratio of one doctor for every 10,000 people.

As the noted African scholar, George H. T. Kimball, has stated: "It is bad enough that a man should be ignorant, for this cuts him off from the commerce of other men's minds. It is perhaps worse that a man should be poor, for this condemns him to a life of stint and scheming, in which there is not time for dreams and no respite from weariness. But what surely is worse is that a man should be unwell, for this prevents him from doing anything much about either his poverty or his ignorance."[1]

Since independence the demand for education in the new nations has increased, with the population of school age continuing to grow at a rate of *5 per cent per year*. In all of Africa, there are more than 30 million children of school age, and only half of these are now in school.

Education has continued to be a dilemma for Africa. The qualitative deficiencies of educational programs aimed at reaching universal primary education by 1980 have resulted in high dropout rates and little real achievement of full literacy —a poor return on an average investment of 25 per cent of recurring, yearly national expenditure. Furthermore, the expansion of the educational system (fed as it is by a surging population growth) has outpaced the rate of economic development, and education has consequently become counterproductive in some ways by creating a group of school dropouts for whom there are insufficient opportunities for productive employment.

New thinking on education in Africa is causing government planners to concentrate on teacher training, technical and vocational education, Africanization of curricula, and, of particular importance, training in agriculture. Recent educational programs have failed to meet the needs of rural people, for they have taught few skills that could actually be related to rural life. Increased vocational education is now considered necessary to meet the need for middle level technicians such as plumbers and electricians. Development experts also foresee a greater need for emphasis on scientific and technical training. In 1965, the UNESCO conference on education held in Lagos, Nigeria, estimated that Africa will need 50,000 to 70,000 more scientists by 1980. At present, there are only 200

[1] George H. T. Kimball, *Tropical Africa*, Vol. II (New York: Twentieth Century Fund, 1960), p. 159.

scientists per million people in Africa as compared to 2,000 per million in Europe.

Africa must make full use of its manpower potential to achieve the increased productivity and the economic growth necessary to keep pace with the rapidly expanding population. This problem is complicated by the fact that African economies already have a high dependency load (the number of people supported by the productivity of each worker). This burden can be expected to grow heavier as the number of children increases because of high birth rates and the old people live longer because of modern medical care. In 1960, 43.1 per cent of the African population was under fifteen years of age, 52.3 per cent was between the ages of fifteen and fifty-nine, and 4.6 per cent was over sixty. Between 1960 and 1965, the population grew at a rate of 2.6 per cent, while the economically active portion of the population grew at a rate of only 1.9 per cent. Therefore, in 1965, the productivity of each worker supported more people than in 1960. Obviously, Africa will be placed temporarily in a severe labor squeeze and must utilize its manpower potential to its fullest capacity.

So far inadequate manpower planning has resulted in a failure to mobilize the African labor force effectively in the development effort. Poor manpower planning results from inadequate data on the African labor force—the size of the labor pool, the location of labor surpluses and deficits, the skills needed, and the skilled workers available. Poor statistical information and a lack of appreciation of the value of information on the characteristics of the population are, at present, unfortunate realities. Employment problems can be seen in five general areas despite a shortage of information: a lack of skilled personnel, a surplus of the educated jobless, low productivity, underemployment, and unemployment.

Ironically, both the shortage of skilled personnel and the surplus of the educated jobless can be related to the previously mentioned failure to attune the educational system to economic realities. The shortage of skilled labor is now found in the technical and managerial sectors of the economy, and by 1985 is also expected to affect agricultural production. The surplus of educated persons without skills that directly relate to economic needs hinders development, for these persons often remain unemployed and thus fail to contribute to the economy. By relying on the traditional welfare system of the extended family for their subsistence, they place an increased burden on that sector of the gainfully employed population which already operates under a high dependency ratio.

Low productivity stems from several factors: poor nutrition, debilitating diseases, inadequate training, and, in urban areas, difficulties experienced by poorly prepared people attempting to cope with new urban situations. Furthermore, the idea of surplus production is alien to many African farmers, for most Africans have led a subsistence existence for centuries. In 1960, it was estimated that three quarters of the African population was engaged in low-productivity agriculture and that half the population lived at a subsistence or near subsistence level. Low productivity in rural areas has been accompanied by underemployment. Seasonal factors create underemployment by leaving many workers idle at certain periods of the year, and subsistence farming without the use of modern farm methods makes much of the available labor force redundant. Underemployment is not unknown in urban areas, where bureaucratic staffs are often swelled with a surplus of educated personnel, as senior personnel are used in capacities that do not correspond to the level of their education.

Underemployment is a problem particularly among the youth in urban areas. Unemployment of youths is due primarily to the failure of young Africans to adjust their aspirations to the economic realities. The young tend to be attracted to urban areas in the hope of finding employment they consider more fitting for their education than agriculture, which still provides work for 75 per cent of the population. Very often they are overeducated for the available job opportunities and underskilled for the employment requirements of existing openings. In North Africa 64.4 per cent, in West Africa 88 per cent, and in East Africa 44.7 per cent of the population aged fifteen through nineteen are not employed.

Unemployment in the urban sector stems from the fact that the rate of urban population growth has far outstripped the increase in employment opportunities. Because urban centers have become symbols of modernity, Africa is experiencing one of the highest urban growth rates in the world, an estimated 5.4 per cent per year. African cities have not had the economic capacity to fill the increasing need of their burgeoning populations for employment as well as social services. Furthermore, statistics indicate that throughout Africa employment opportunities have not expanded as quickly as the population. In the developing nations of Africa between 1960 and 1965 the rate of employment slowed and in some nations the level of employment fell. Industrialization has expanded at a faster rate than the accompanying rate of employment. For example, between 1958 and 1962 industrial output in the United Arab Republic doubled, while employment only rose by 6 per cent. In Kenya, Rhodesia, Tanzania, and Zambia output has increased while employment has remained about the same. Africa's concentration on capital-intensive industries and significant increases in productivity through the introduction of technology have resulted in the slow rate of expansion for employment.

Housing is one critical area where the pressure of a rapidly expanding population, particularly in urban areas, is severely taxing the ability of African economies to keep pace. Insufficient attention has been given to housing in relation to over-all development plans. Although there are no reliable statistics available on housing in Africa, present plans call for housing data to be included in the 1970 censuses. Estimates by the United Nations Economic Commission on Africa (ECA) indicate that the present rate of construction of new urban residential units in Africa south of the Sahara is only one third of what is needed. UN development experts believe there is an annual need for ten new housing units per thousand population and that currently only two units per thousand are being constructed. The West African sub-region, with a population of approximately 100 million, has an estimated housing need of 240,000 new units per year. Some areas in East Africa are also confronted with a housing crisis. In Nairobi, Kenya, the city council plans to build 2,000 new residential units per year. At present, city housing projects in Nairobi have a waiting list of over 25,000.

Africa's hopes for economic progress that will ease the threat of population pressure depend upon agriculture more than any other single factor. Current estimates place the agricultural growth rate of Africa at 2.4 per cent per year, while the population is increasing by 2.6 per cent per year. Because food production has increased by only 1.6 per cent per year, many African nations spend precious foreign exchange on costly food imports instead of utilizing revenues for such developments as schools, roads, and public utilities. More important, poor progress in agriculture acts as a depressant upon the whole economy. Like the Western industrial revolution, Africa's future industrialization depends upon the development of an agricultural income base. Not only do three quarters of Africa's people depend upon agriculture for their livelihood, but approximately 35 per cent of Africa's gross domestic product stems from agricultural production.

African agriculture is characterized by extremely low productivity. Subsistence agriculture accounts for approximately 50 per cent of the output. Traditional methods of farming utilizing family labor are widespread, though agricultural extension services and land tenure schemes aim at developing a large cadre of progressive farmers. It is estimated that 92 per cent of the land in Africa is subject to some climatic disability that affects its agricultural potential. In many areas the soil

tends to be very poor and susceptible to erosion and deple-
tion. Extremes in rainfall from year to year add to Africa's
agricultural problems. Increased agricultural production in
rural areas would be possible through more effective land
distribution and land use. However, in certain areas cultural
factors such as tribalism work against the most efficient use of
fertile land areas. For example, in Kenya the pastoral Masai
tribe possesses some land that is underpopulated and culti-
vatable. As herdsmen, however, the Masai have little liking
for agriculture. On the other hand, the Kikuyu, who are
more agriculturally oriented and who make up almost 20 per
cent of the country's population, live on a disproportionately
small segment of the nation's territory.

Cultural patterns and attitudes also perpetuate low productivity in other ways. For example, in certain ethnic groups
women are traditionally assigned the function of cultivation,
and a social stigma is attached to active work in agriculture by
a man. This hinders any effort to increase agricultural productivity by mobilizing the energies of the men in the community. In areas where this attitude prevails there is little
likelihood that agricultural potentials will be realized as long
as the women make up the main labor force. Unless the situation changes, the people will continue to live on a subsistence
basis.

Not only is a regard for traditional African custom important in development areas such as agriculture, but it is also
crucial in planning programs for population control. Kinship
ties, tribes and extended family units, are the warp and woof
of the fabric of African society. While modernization is occurring, many Africans still derive their identity from their
relationship to their communal groups. Planners must therefore be sensitive to the relationship between birth control and
African attitudes toward family units if they are to convince
citizens of the connection between population control, economic progress, and an increased standard of living.

Sound development is greatly needed if Africa is to achieve

adequate economic growth. A recent report of the United Nations Economic Commission on Africa observed that "spontaneous growth on the required scale, is, however probably impossible; and it could be argued that growth and development will proceed from planning or not at all."[2] National economic planning has been a fairly widely accepted concept in Africa; approximately thirty countries have adopted national development plans. However, it is disturbing to note that many of these plans have failed to provide sufficiently for or anticipate population growth. Africa must create an economic structure able to support a population that will triple in the next thirty-one years.

A lack of accurate population data is perhaps the greatest impediment to careful consideration of population factors in development planning. Many African countries rely on administrative censuses to determine population size and distribution. These are reports of village headmen or tax counts—usually grossly underestimated. "In cases where these administrative censuses have been followed by complete enumerations, the earlier censuses have been found to have underenumerated the population by as much as 20 per cent."[3]

Africa must recognize the importance of the study of population and its characteristics as a social discipline, and the importance of this discipline, demography, as a tool in economic development plans. Without a greater understanding of the phenomena of population, the newly created African nations face insurmountable obstacles politically, socially, and economically. Solving human problems requires, first, understand-

[2] Economic Commission for Africa, *Economic Conditions in Africa in Recent Years*, 9th session, Addis Ababa, February 3-14, 1969 (E/CN. 14/435), p. 164.
[3] Unpublished background paper for East and West Africa regional conferences on population for Agency for International Development mission officials, August, 1967. Prepared by Manpower and Research Division, Population Service, Office of the War on Hunger, AID, Washington, D.C. From a paper presented at the World Population Conference, Belgrade, Yugoslavia, 1965.

ing the extent of human need. Imagine how difficult it would be to deal with our own problems of housing, transportation, food distribution, and health without knowing the size of the population, the rate of population growth, and the estimated population in given areas over the next ten years. In Africa there are at best poor estimates of population size, and usually no estimates of birth and death rates or the age distribution of populations. Economic development plans in Africa, as a result, are "guesstimates" of population needs.

The population picture in Africa is not all bleak, however, and the first step in recognizing the importance of population characteristics in economic development plans has been taken. The United Nations Economic Commission for Africa was asked by the African countries to make a review and report on the present status of population in Africa. An initial report was recently prepared, and in March, 1968, a demographic handbook of Africa was published. Other worthwhile research on the population of Africa has been published recently by various private organizations and universities. But much more needs to be done. A great deal could be done if the African nations would request technical advisory assistance in the development of national population policies. Only five African countries signed a recent UN General Assembly resolution on population growth and economic development. Only four African countries have adopted policies aimed at reducing population growth, and to date only fourteen other countries have sponsored unofficial family planning programs.

Although the first step has been taken, it has been a small step. More effort to expand knowledge of population problems will enable African governments to cope better with many pressing economic problems. Present efforts to introduce population studies in African schools are only token efforts. The United States and other countries could make important contributions to this effort through assistance in institutional development. Such long-range assistance will pay off decades from now if the right policy decisions have been made. The need is for the United States to recognize the pressing population problems in Africa and to begin *now* to provide long-range institutional support. Assistance in this area should be for the establishment of research facilities and for the development of staff to teach and conduct the necessary research. For example, medical schools should be assisted in the development of courses of study in population dynamics and research.

Other areas of assistance should not be neglected in favor of statistical studies or family planning services. It is important to understand that in population studies and in dealing with population problems, as in any other development endeavor, the approach must be a total approach considering all aspects of the development effort. One mistake we have made in the United States in the past is that of failing to realize that assistance in one needed area is not—and cannot be—the answer to all ills. An example is our aid in public health programs in Africa, which is motivated by sound humanitarian principles. Though the elimination of communicable diseases such as malaria, smallpox, and measles is without question desirable, what of the effects on the balance of population in Africa? They are potentially disastrous.

Generally speaking, high mortality is common among people with a low standard of living, inadequate education, and a scarcity of medical and public health services and facilities. In Africa, historically, epidemics, a poorly balanced diet, and intertribal warfare have contributed to the high mortality rate. When one principal factor contributing to high mortality is reduced or even eliminated, the whole balance between births and deaths and the size and age distribution of the population are drastically changed. In Africa the mortality rate is dropping, and more children are being brought into the world and raised to adulthood than ever before. The decline in mortality has been accelerated with the introduction of intensive public health programs designed to reduce diseases which normally act to balance the population size. In the meantime birth rates, reinforced by strong cultural norms, continue to be high. We have then, in Africa, the threat of a birth-death rate imbalance, which promises to confound all efforts to achieve a sustained trend toward economic growth and political and social stability.

There are, to be sure, positive factors favoring continuation of medical assistance, and I do not want to imply any opposition to public health assistance. For that matter, my impression is that medical assistance can be one of the most effective measures yet employed to assist economic development. The question I raise is that of emphasis and balance. For example, assistance in the care of mothers and children, long denied to the Africans, would reduce infant mortality, raise life expectancy, and generally improve the well-being of the African family. Public health assistance to reduce the incidence of diseases is greatly desired. It has long been accepted as a fact of life that the apparent lethargy, passiveness, and despair so evident among poor people everywhere results in part from the prevalence of disease. Reducing disease, and therefore improving the energies and productive capacities of the people, will have a tremendous impact on the productivity and vitality of the economy, a most desirable goal. On the other hand, merely reducing disease and in this way reducing mortality will not in the long run have the impact we desire. Housing shortages, underemployment problems, the need for improved agriculture techniques, and so forth, are common in every developing economy. In Africa these problems may become impossible to solve given the problem of the present population growth rate. Thus the obvious critical need to bring the birth-death ratios into balance.

As the African nations move toward urbanization, can we expect large families to become an economic liability and can we expect the people to lower birth rates voluntarily? One report points out the negative factors of the problems in the following discussion:[4]

Nevertheless, while we can expect the death rate to decline rapidly, we cannot anticipate an equivalent decline in African birth rates and annual increase rates in the near future. Some modern influences are likely to offset any fertility declines which other influences foster. Improved health programs are likely to increase fecundity and child health. The development of maternity hospitals will undoubtedly raise the proportion of live births and improve postnatal care for mother as well as child. Education threatens to eradicate a traditional custom of abstaining from sexual intercourse during a two-year lactation period after the birth of each child, a custom which has served to keep the birth rate lower than it might have been. Finally, growing prosperity may buttress the large family custom by making support of more children more feasible. One author has placed the appearance of any birth rate decline in tropical Africa after 1980. (Etienne van de Walle, "Future Growth of Population and Changes of Population Composition: Tropical Africa," *Proceedings of the World Population Conference*, Vol. II, p. 156.) The necessary restructuring of cultural values, barely evident elsewhere, has not even begun in the tropical zone. Every African government gives other development programs higher priority than population planning. In fact, officials in many countries, if they are aware of all of the warnings of population experts, tend to suspect these warnings as white imperialist efforts to curb the increase of black populations. Eventual restoration of a balance between the birth and death rates may occur, but will it occur soon enough? Many obstacles to such a balance must first be overcome.

Today Africa is the continent with the world's lowest population density. Africa is not overpopulated and is not

[4] Unpublished background paper for East and West Africa regional conference on population for Agency for International Development mission officials, Kampala, Uganda, and Monrovia, Liberia, August, 1967. Prepared by Manpower and Research Division, Population Service, office of the War on Hunger, Agency for International Development, Washington, D.C.

threatened with overpopulation. Why, then, is its population problem so critical in relation to economic development? The answer is that density is insignificant in a consideration of overpopulation. In Africa the crucial population problem is not the average number of people per square mile on that continent, but, depending upon the area we are talking about, how many people can an area accommodate adequately and still progress economically and socially. The critical factors are the availability of resources in a given area and the extent of their development to support a population.

The emergence of African nation-states marks the end of an era of colonial empires. Today Africa is going through the complex transformations of nation-building and technological revolution. Ultimately Africa's future place in world affairs will depend upon how successful it is in coming to grips with its development problems. It remains for the United States and other developed nations to assist Africans in achieving a sustained rise in economic growth. This is most important, for the destiny of this diverse continent depends upon the measure of internal political stability achieved in the next decade. Such stability will only come through the mobilizing forces of a people striving for mutually advantageous economic goals.

Africa has been called the *last* frontier in world affairs. Through vital technical advice and assistance in agricultural development, comprehensive public health services, and an appreciation of the impact of population phenomena on development endeavors, the United States and other developed nations of the world can contribute greatly to the future prospects of Africa. We can help it to become a *new* frontier for economic co-operation and development. Africa's assets can be its people, diversity, size, and natural resources. The rest of the world can help Africa take advantage of these assets.

6

Latin America: Eliminating Human Misery

IN 1965, Dr. Alberto Lleras Camargo, one of the Western Hemisphere's most distinguished statesman, testified before the Senate Subcommittee on Foreign Aid Expenditures regarding Latin America's population growth. Dr. Lleras, former secretary general of the Organization of American States and former president of Colombia, warned that, at the speed at which Latin America's population has been growing, the problem

is beyond manageable proportions, and certainly beyond the capacities of the Latin Americans to cope with it. Latin America is breeding misery, revolutionary pressures, famine and many other potentially disastrous problems in proportions that exceed our imagination even in the age of thermonuclear war.

During the 1967 Christmas recess of Congress, I visited Argentina, Brazil, Chile, and Peru. Before the trip I was familiar with the statistical evidence of the deplorable living conditions in the region: the high infant mortality rates, huge housing shortages, low per-capita income, large numbers of children for whom there are no educational facilities, and other indicators of underdevelopment.

But cold statistics do not convey the human suffering they represent. Visits to the *cayampas, barriadas,* and *favelas,* choking Latin America's urban centers, showed me with terrible vividness the misery and degradation endured by millions of people in what we often fondly refer to as "our sister Republics." The sight also made painfully clear the staggering developmental tasks confronting the Latin American people—tasks made infinitely more difficult, if not impossible, by the tidal wave of new lives entering the scene each year and claiming a share of the already precarious subsistence available.

I came away convinced that Dr. Lleras had diagnosed Latin America's situation without emotionalism, without exaggeration, and without dramatic embellishment. There is simply no way to discuss the impact of Latin America's elevated birth rates without a theatrical sense of urgency.

Latin America's population problem is massive and foreboding; like a Greek tragedy, it seems to be rolling inexorably toward catastrophe. The population is multiplying at a phenomenal rate, faster than the economies can provide the basic sustenance for decent lives. It is difficult for me to believe that democracy can long survive in any nation with a population increase greater than 1.5 per cent.

With our domestic problems crying for solutions, it would be comforting to slough off concern about the ominous trends in Latin America, to concentrate our energies and treasury on our own troubles and let the Latin Americans worry about theirs.

But there are considerations, apart from our humanitarian instincts, that counsel against such a course. The United States cannot hope to exist as a peaceful, prosperous island in a rising sea of impoverished, unstable nations. A chaotic Latin America, convulsed either by mindless upheaval and revolution or by sinister intent, could have serious repercussions upon the security of the United States.

It is imperative that we understand the gravity of Latin America's population problem and the urgency of initiating a major effort to assist the Latin Americans in their economic development efforts.

Latin America's population growth rate, 3 per cent a year, is the highest among the regions of the world. (Only Argentina and Uruguay have a reasonable rate of growth.)

The continent's population has grown rapidly only in the last few decades. The spectacular increases are the result of a combination of declines in mortality rates, thanks to modern medicine (largely from the United States), some minor advances in environmental sanitation, and a continuation of traditionally high birth rates. The growth rate continues to edge upward as a steadily growing population base yields more births.

Latin America's population in 1960 was 213 million. If the present growth trend continues, the population will reach 690 million by the end of the century.[1] In other words, in only four decades Latin America will have to absorb another 477 million people, or much more than double the present population of the United States.

With only about 9 people per square kilometer, Latin America has a population density about half that of the United States and only one tenth that of Europe. The low population density and large masses of uninhabited land on the continent are often cited by some Latin politicians as evidence that Latin America has no population problem, but rather needs *more* people to develop its resources. For example, during a debate in Brazil in August, 1966, over the possibility of U.S. aid on population problems, Dr. Fabio Fonseca, president of the Belo Horizonte Regional Council of Medicine, stated that Brazil needs a population twice its

[1] Agency for International Development, Office of the War on Hunger, *Population Program Assistance* (Washington, D.C., September 1968), p. 64.

present size in order to settle the vast empty spaces of the country.[2]

Inaugurating a meeting of ministers of public health of the Americas in October, 1968, Lieutenant General Juan Carlos Ongañia, president of Argentina, declared:[3]

In no case has progress and development been achieved with selfish and suicidal criteria, but with energy, generosity and creative spirit. History teaches that curbing life leads to decadency. If America wishes to fulfill its destiny of being the continent of the future, it must not artificially restrain the human resources which have to carry out that calling.

Those urging the-more-the-merrier concept apparently believe that additional people mean additional muscle and brain power. In this vein, a Brazilian minister of health told the World Health Organization in March 1964:[4]

In underdeveloped countries such as Brazil, where over 50 per cent of the energy utilized in production is muscular in nature, population size constitutes a real element of power which is the most important means of national progress. Therefore, anything which increases growth is beneficial for us.

Peru's ambassador to the United Nations argued in the UN Population Commission in 1962:[5]

Can we know the mystery of unborn men, who might have brought a new message for humanity? The greatest capital is the inventive genius of man.

[2] Samuel Clark Thornburg, "Is Population Growth a Deterrent to the Development of Latin America?" (Agency for International Development, Washington, D.C., [n.d.], mimeo), p. 9.
[3] *Discurso del Presidente de la Nación al inaugurar la reunión especial de Ministros de Salud Pública de las Americas.* Copy on file at Library of Congress, Legislative Reference Service, Foreign Affairs Division.
[4] J. Mayone Stycos, *Human Fertility in Latin America* (Ithaca, N.Y.: Cornell University Press, 1968), p. 39.
[5] Ibid., p. 40.

Other Latin Americans contend that the region requires a large population to provide cheap labor and consumers for large-scale industries.

Advocates of large populations in Latin America fail to distinguish between population size and density and the rate of population growth. It is the latter, the high and progressively rising rate of population growth, that is the essence of Latin America's population problem.

Latin America does possess large tracts of virtually uninhabited land and potential mineral resources the extent of which are not known. However, the crucial scarcities hampering development are capital and skills, not people. In this respect, Mr. Stycos, an astute student of the area, notes:[6]

Those who point to wide open spaces as evidence for the need for more population might ask themselves the question: Why are there so few people there now? It is hardly the case that Latin Americans do not like to move, or are irrational about economically advantageous settlement. Since World War II migration from rural areas to the crowded cities has been phenomenal. . . . The flight is *away* from the wide open spaces. And with good reason. Migration to the city represents an easier and more pleasant readjustment than migration to a new rural area, and is a better risk for social and economic improvement. To get people to move to rural areas requires patience, skill, and capital. . . . The only point in settling new areas is to *increase* agricultural productivity. . . . But *more* population is not needed for this purpose. There are already too many people on unproductive lands. . . . The situation can be remedied either by adding capital, skills, and improved organization to existing lands, or by removing excess rural population to more productive lands.

Latin America's dilemma is that it is direly short of capital and skills. And it is the region's spectacular population growth that is the principal obstacle to acquiring both these essential ingredients for progress.

[6] Ibid., p. 25.

Sufficient capital resources can only come from a broad national savings program, that is, from earnings over and above what is needed for immediate consumption. Outside investment and aid supply only a small portion; in Latin America, about 87 per cent of total gross investment is financed from domestic savings.

Larger populations will not automatically generate greater amounts of capital. On the contrary, Latin America's population growth causes an increasing shortage of funds available for promoting economic development. The damaging effect of the region's accelerated population growth is threefold:

First, high rates of population growth require higher proportions of national income to be saved and invested merely to maintain current levels of per capita income.

Second, the region's soaring growth has loaded the population with a high proportion of unproductive young, about 43 per cent fifteen years of age and younger. This large number of dependent children requires a rising government investment in services, especially education and health, which reduces the capacity of the public sector to save and invest in tangible productive assets and also implies increased taxes with a decreased taxable source.

Third, by limiting availability of capital, rapid population growth impedes the opening and developing of new areas, thus channeling migrations of the rural poor toward urban areas. These massive migrations have placed staggering burdens upon the health, education, sanitation, housing, and transportation facilities of Latin American cities.

Tragically, the Latin American countries are extremely hard-pressed just to keep services on a par with population increases, let alone to make improvements.

Clearly, the economic development of a country is dependent not only on the quantity but also on the quality of its human resources. The financial burden of educating the ever-increasing number of youngsters is far heavier in high-fertility countries than in countries with low birth rates. In effect, the high-fertility countries have to run harder just to keep from falling behind.

According to the latest available data, about 33 per cent of the Latin American people are illiterate. While this compares favorably with the percentages in other underdeveloped regions (the Near East, 74 per cent; South Asia, 75 per cent; Africa, 80 per cent), it is high in comparison with the illiteracy rates of 4 per cent in member countries of the European Common Market and 2.4 per cent in the United States. Yet, despite progress in raising the literacy rate, the number of adult illiterates is still increasing.

The Alliance for Progress set a goal of providing at least elementary education for all children. Between 1960 and 1967, secondary school enrollment increased by about 50 per cent, the number of teachers by 61 per cent, and the number of classrooms by 51 per cent. In more than half the participating countries, primary schools now are graduating at least twice as many students a year as they did at the beginning of the Alliance, and the remaining countries have also reported increases in the annual number of graduates. In all, 2.7 million children graduated from primary school in 1967 as compared with only 1.5 million in 1960.

Despite these relatively laudable accomplishments, the number of children for whom there are *no* schools is growing each year. And the situation promises to deteriorate.

In 1967 the population of Latin America aged seven through fourteen was about 52.9 million. About 34.3 million, or 64.8 per cent, of these attended school, while some 18.6 million were not in school. At present fertility rates, by 1997 the population in this elementary school age group will reach 135.2 million, an increase of 155 per cent in only thirty years.[7] In order to maintain just the percentage of children now in school, it would be necessary for Latin America to

[7] Unpublished paper, "United States Policy Toward Latin American Population Growth," p. 28.

provide buildings and to train and pay teachers for 87.6 million children by 1997. Even if this monumental task could be accomplished, the number of children for whom there would be no schooling in 1997 would rise to 47.6 million.[8] Hence, if the present population growth rate continues, in only thirty years the number of children destined to grow up illiterate and untrained will more than double.

Under such conditions, the swelling labor force is not being equipped with the necessary skills to contribute to the productive capacity of the economy. In short, high fertility is expanding the supply of labor while debasing its quality. Moreover, since wages to unskilled labor will continue to fall relative to the returns on capital and skills, these circumstances can only intensify existing social inequities.

Probably no element on the Latin American scene presents more visible evidence of the impact of the pace of population growth than housing conditions. Forty per cent of the region's urban population, about 45 million people, live under extremely crowded conditions, with three or more persons per room in units made of improvised materials.

In Central America, only about 17 per cent of the urban population live in houses connected to sewage systems; in South America, about 49 per cent.[9] In rural areas, it is estimated that less than 10 per cent of the homes have running water and sanitary facilities, and the remaining 90 per cent are mud and wattle shacks or adobe huts, which have changed very little since pre-Columbian times.[10]

The *favelas* of Recife, in northeast Brazil, were as ugly and depressing as any slums I saw in South America. They have been described by some as the worst in the world, not exclud-

[8] Ibid.
[9] Abraham Horwitz and Mary H. Burke, "Health, Population and Development," in J. Mayone Stycos and Jorge Arias, eds., *Population Dilemma in Latin America* (Washington, D.C., Potomac Books, Inc., 1966), p. 176.
[10] Inter-American Development Bank, Social Progress Trust Fund, Sixth Annual Report, 1966, p. 31.

ing those in China before World War II and those in India today. The houses are built on wooden stilts over marsh, mud, and water, and raw sewage is dumped directly into the ditches and tributaries below. The people are packed into their homes like sardines.

In Peru, in the *barriada* Augustino, built on the side of a mountain in Lima, I saw the sewage running down open streets between the houses, with everything from foraging pigs and chickens to dead dogs in the running water. Yet, according to the young Peace Corps volunteers with whom I visited in Peru, the residents of Lima's *barriadas*, Andean Indians who have swarmed down from the bleak altiplano, feel that their migration to the city is a step forward. They have a sense of hope—for a better job, for an opportunity in the future for a child to go to school. The Peace Corps workers also pointed out that there is presently no violent crime problem. That would come, they felt, in another ten, twelve, or fifteen years if the population growth problem is not ameliorated. If the *barriada* residents cannot find jobs, if they cannot get food, if their children begin to starve, the mood could change radically.

It has been estimated that the housing shortage in Latin America is some 15 million units and that the cost of providing these units would exceed $23.5 billion. An additional 1.4 million units are required annually to meet population growth and replacement needs.[11] Despite record-breaking building activity under the auspices of the Alliance for Progress, less than one-half million dwellings are being constructed annually. Thus, the deficit increases by about one million housing units each year. And no dent is made in the backlog.

Education and housing are but two of the many vital sectors where the rapid population increase is taking its toll. When population pressures are discussed, the main topic that

[11] Inter-American Development Bank, Social Progress Trust Fund, Fourth Annual Report, 1964.

usually arises is food production, perhaps because of the Malthusian theory of overpopulation resulting in famine.

"Latin America," Congressman Henry S. Reuss warned in a 1967 report, "is rapidly approaching a Malthusian crisis."[12] However, he went on, "This grim picture of Latin American agricultural stagnation is not an inevitable picture."[13]

Other competent observers, while they do not see a Malthusian crisis as imminent, do at least agree that excessive population growth and lagging food supply are having dire repercussions on Latin American economic and social progress.

Agricultural production has kept only slightly ahead of population growth during the past fifteen years. The lag in output is particularly significant because nearly 50 per cent of the labor force earn their livelihood from farming, and agriculture will continue to be a cornerstone of the region's economy for some time. Output per man in agriculture is only a third that of industry or in service occupations. This results in extremely low levels of rural income, which are reflected in inadequate diets and poor housing, sanitation, and health, and in turn spark the mass exodus from rural areas to urban center.

The industrial sector in Latin America offers few opportunities for the rural immigrants. While industry employs more people than it did a decade ago, the high urban population growth has more than offset the increase in jobs. Despite massive migration to urban areas, the number of people living in rural areas continues to grow. Thus, agricultural underemployment and its concomitant, rural poverty, remain.

To meet the requirements of a rapidly expanding population, the increased demand engendered by increased incomes, and the rising level of exports, it has been estimated by the

[12] U.S. Congress, House, Committee on Banking and Currency, *Food for Progress in Latin America*, by Henry S. Reuss, Chairman, Subcommittee on International Finance, 89th Cong., 2d sess., February 8, 1967, p. 1.
[13] Ibid., p. 3.

Alliance representatives at the Punta del Este, Uruguay, meeting in August, 1961, that the total agricultural output should grow by 5 per cent a year in Latin America. This rate would be higher if the need to improve currently low nutritional levels were taken into account.[14] Since the beginning of the Alliance for Progress, net agricultural production has increased on the average of about 3 per cent a year, well below target.[15]

And what about the region's nutritional levels, which are not even included in the Alliance goal? Per-capita food supply in most Latin American countries is unsatisfactory. This is particularly true of such "protective" foods as meat, vegetables, eggs, fish, milk, and fats and oils. Average per-capita availability of calories and, especially, of proteins, fats, and certain minerals and vitamins, is substantially below internationally accepted minimum nutritional standards.[16]

The results of this lack of proper nutrients are apathy, lethargy, and lack of initiative, all of which erode human productivity. Malnutrition also lowers a worker's resistance to disease, thereby increasing his rate of absenteeism. Malnutrition reduces life expectancy, limiting a man's productive years. Morever, as was emphasized in 1969 in hearings before Senator George McGovern's Senate Select Committee on Nutrition and Human Needs, malnutrition of mothers during pregnancy and of children during the first several years of life permanently impairs the children's ability to learn. The vicious circle is joined; poverty results in undernourishment, which creates unproductivity, which results in poverty.

With its food production growing more slowly than the number of people to be fed, Latin America has been forced to import huge quantities of food just to maintain present woe-

14 Inter-American Development Bank, Social Progress Trust Fund, Sixth Annual Report, p. 42.
15 U.S. Department of State, Bureau of Inter-American Affairs, *Latin American Growth Trends* (April 1968), p. 16.
16 Inter-American Development Bank, op. cit., p. 43.

ful dietary levels. Food imports from outside the region already amount to over $600 million a year (this is $600 million not available for education, services, or capital investment).

The situation has severe repercussions on the region's economic and social development. Expenditure of scarce foreign exchange for food imports reduces the funds available to buy capital goods and other requirements for modernization. At the same time, expanding domestic consumption depletes the quantity of food products for export, and it also decreases the amount of foreign exchange available for investment purposes.

Many observers agree that the problem could be solved by a massive expansion of food production in Latin America, to be accomplished by bringing new lands into production and by greatly increasing productivity on existing arable land.

However, the prospects for a dramatic boost in the region's agricultural output are not reassuring. A superficial look at the map of Latin America gives a deceptive impression regarding agricultural possibilities. There are indeed huge expanses of relatively vacant land. But most of the space that appears so tantalizing on the map has not attracted settlement for good reasons. It includes some of the world's most rugged, snow-capped mountains, barren deserts, and dense tropical rain forests.

To open those areas would entail expenditures for such costly improvements as mountain road networks and irrigation facilities. These would impose an enormous drain on budgets already hard pressed by countless other demands. The costs could be justified only in relation to the benefits to be derived.

In this respect, it must be noted that colonizing new areas does not automatically bring an increase in agricultural productivity. When colonization projects are far from their markets, commerce is limited and sometimes impossible. Self-sufficient agricultural colonies neither improve the prosperity of the farmer nor contribute to the national agricultural supply. Further, if the factors now hampering production—such as the prevailing poor land tenure systems, poor farming techniques, marketing bottlenecks, and price-cost ratios geared to favor city dwellers—are transferred to the new areas, the expensive projects would result merely in expanding the number of people engaged in unproductive agriculture.

As for colonizing the tropics, those seemingly endless expanses in the heartland of the continent, a serious impediment exists. The few people who do farm in Latin America's immense rain forests usually practice slash-and-burn agriculture. They cut down a stand of trees, burn the trees and shrubs, cultivate the plot for a year or two until torrential rains have leached the soil of nutrients, and then move on to repeat the process elsewhere. Of this seemingly primitive practice, the report of a six-week conference on agricultural problems in underdeveloped countries, sponsored jointly by AID and the Massachusetts Institute of Technology, states:[17]

The conference was impressed by the great areas in which our knowledge is so limited that little if anything can be done. The soils of the tropical rain forests are an example; present knowledge does not seem to provide an alternative to the existing methods of cultivation. Only much fuller understanding of rain-forest ecology, demanding a long-term research effort, would make possible a substantial advance in production.

In short, the world does not presently possess the kind of information or expertise essential to convert Latin America's tropical forests into productive farms.

Belatedly, the need for research in tropical agriculture is being recognized. Studies are being inaugurated or are underway in several places in Latin America, including a tropical agricultural research station near Cali, Colombia, financed

[17] Massachusetts Institute of Technology, Center for International Studies, *Policies for Promoting Agricultural Development: Report of a Conference on Productivity and Innovation in Agriculture in Underdeveloped Countries* (June 1965), p. 53.

jointly by the Ford, Rockefeller, and Kellogg Foundations. Not nearly enough is being done, however, to provide a sound basis for improved tropical agricultural production.

Unhappily, the time lag between experimentation and application of new technology can be excruciatingly long. Hence, opening new areas for settlement does not hold short range promise as a solution to Latin America's food problem.

This leaves the alternative short-term course, greatly increasing productivity on existing arable land, while building up institutional capability to promote long-range tropical agriculture research. Of Latin America's prospects in this respect, Professor William C. Thiesenhusen of Wisconsin's Land Tenure Center has made the following comments:[18]

The United States achieved rapid increases in yield per acre beginning about 1940. But we should remember that it took decades to set the stage for the productivity revolution here. By the time our frontier closed and intensive farming became necessary, we had an established freehold system, a backlog of agricultural research results, well-developed State and local governments, an active extension service, widespread literacy, and adequate communications networks.

Most countries in Latin America are trying to make the transformation to intensive agriculture in a much different context. The task before them is unprecedented—to modernize agriculture despite the fact that agricultural research is as yet inadequate, illiteracy is widespread, inputs are scarce, product markets are weak, and the institutional framework of agriculture is faulty.

In view of these stark realities, it is wishful thinking to count upon a substantial leap in Latin America's agricultural production to meet the requirements of its burgeoning population over the next few years.

"If present birth rates continue," warns Professor Thiesenhusen, "overpopulation will doom all effort to achieve food

[18] U.S., Congress, Senate, Committee on Foreign Relations, Subcommittee on South American Republics Affairs, *Survey of the Alliance for Progress: Hearings*, 90th Cong., 2d sess., 1968, p. 5.

balance."[19] A strong effort in support of nationwide birth control programs by the various governments will buy time for the Latin American people. Then through tropical agriculture research they can improve the yield of their crops and learn about how to properly use and maintain the soils of the tropics and subtropics.

The Alliance for Progress was designed to end the tragic conditions prevailing in much of Latin America. The Charter of the Alliance, adopted at Punta del Este in August, 1961, by the United States and nineteen Latin American countries (all the members of the Organization of American States except Cuba), proclaimed the decision of the American Republics "to unite in a common effort to bring our people accelerated economic progress and broader social justice within the framework of personal dignity and political liberty."

The Alliance has promoted some notable achievements. For example, tax reforms have resulted in a significant increase in the tax receipts of most of the nineteen Latin American participants—an increase of more than 50 per cent in eight countries since the Alliance's inception and between 30 and 50 per cent in five others. About 1,800 potable water systems, serving over 10 million people, have been built. Thousands of classrooms have also been built and primary school enrollment has been boosted by 23 per cent, secondary school enrollment by 50 per cent, and university enrollment by 40 per cent.

Yet the Alliance for Progress has disappointed many, including its most ardent supporters. Despite self-help measures and foreign aid, Latin America has been unable to make substantial progress.

The situation is like the nightmare of a long-distance runner, in which he runs and runs only to find that the finish line keeps moving ahead another mile. Many of the Latin American nations have exerted considerable effort to achieve Alli-

[19] Ibid., p. 4.

ance for Progress objectives, only to see their goals recede as phenomenal increases in population multiply requirements for housing, food, education, jobs, health facilities, transport, and other services.

Some, disheartened by Latin America's rate of progress, are inclined to write off the Alliance for Progress as a failure. I believe, on the contrary, that the concepts of the Alliance remain valid. The tax, land, educational, and other reforms called for by the Charter of Punta del Este are vital to the promotion of economic and social justice in the region. Foreign, technical, and financial assistance continues to be of indispensable support for Latin America's self-help measures.

What has been missing from the Alliance is a realization of the deadening effect of the region's high birth rates upon all efforts to achieve economic and social progress and a consequent determination to remove that barrier to development.

Of course, other factors have conspired to restrict progress under the Alliance. Prominent among these are the dearth of competent administrators and technicians; lack of institutional bases, such as agricultural extension services; and a trained civil service, through which assistance could be funneled; resistance to change on the part of privileged groups;* and political systems too fragile to survive if reforms alienate influential sectors.

Despite these inherent obstacles, sufficient advances have been made under the aegis of the Alliance for Progress to indicate that the program has merit. But the gains are being obscured by Latin America's soaring population increase.

By the mid 1960's a very, very faint glimmer of hope for a rational solution seemed to appear. Latin American physicians began to compare notes and to speak out about the horrendous number of induced abortions in their countries. At the

---

* Author's note: In Peru 80–90 per cent of the land is owned by approximately 2 per cent of the people.

same time, Latin American economists, frustrated by the slow economic and social gains achieved under the Alliance for Progress, became increasingly aware of and alarmed by the implications of population growth.

As more and more Latin Americans of eminence spoke out on the formerly taboo subject of birth control, the view that contraception was too sensitive a matter for government consideration began to weaken in some quarters. The traditionally cautious Organization of American States held a symposium on population problems in 1964, and the following year they appointed a special committee to consider demographic questions.

In a few years overt official opposition in Latin America to any action on birth control declined. Beginning in 1964 some form of public and private family planning activities and related studies were emerging in most countries. Although strong opposition largely disappeared, active government assistance has meant that whatever programs are established have little significant impact on the population.

In the same period, policy in the United States also shifted. Formerly, it was generally assumed that government had no proper role to play in population matters, and men in public life shunned discussion of what was regarded as a purely personal matter.

In his first message on foreign aid in 1961, President John F. Kennedy, speaking about the problem of development, said: "The magnitude of the problem is really staggering. In Latin America, for example, population growth is already threatening to outpace economic growth—and in some parts of the continent, living standards are actually declining." At the time, however, the President made no policy recommendations, and when the American Republics met at Punta del Este to devise a charter for the Alliance for Progress, the issue of Latin America's growing population was not even raised. Rather, the architects of the Charter assumed that modernization of Latin American societies by means of the proposed regional program would automatically provide for their escalating populations.

During this time the U.S. leadership began to move forward with population policies, beginning with the U.S. Congress's initiative in 1963 authorizing funds for population research in the Foreign Assistance Act. Then following President Johnson's statement of new policy toward population growth in his 1965 State of the Union message, the Congress passed population legislation in 1966 and the following year earmarked funds for population programs. This flurry of U.S. activity was matched very modestly by the South American governments. What progress was made came primarily through local private efforts and private international organizations such as the International Planned Parenthood Federation (IPPF). A start has been made but not nearly enough to be even mildly optimistic. Strong official government support in Latin America is needed before a truly reasonable attack can be made on population growth rates.

The minimum changes of official attitudes toward birth control have not occurred without opposition. Willingness of the United States to co-operate with Latin American countries in establishing birth control programs has aroused much suspicion and protest in the region.

For the Latin American nationalist, every move the United States makes automatically has an "imperialist" motive. According to Colombian Professor Herman Vergara, the United States motive is to prevent Latin America from acquiring a human potential equivalent to that of China and becoming a powerful rival at our border.[20]

A Brazilian is quoted as saying that population control was being "imposed on us by a country with the dimensions of Brazil but with 300 [sic] million people, giving the impression

[20] Newton Carlos, "La 'píldora' in el continente," *Ercilla*, No. 1732, 28 de Agosto–3 de Septiembre, 1968, p. 30.

that the American people, with their land already overpopulated, is concerning itself with our empty spaces and intends
to occupy our territory."[21]

Many Latin American intellectuals who have been profoundly influenced by Marxist ideology deny that population
can be a problem in a well-run economy. They regard birth
control programs as a tactic to divert attention from the
necessity for economic and social reform and as capitalism's
last hope for preserving the status quo. Others, while conced-
ing that population growth is a problem, believe it is the kind
of irritant needed to force basic reforms in the economic and
social structure. Radimiro Tomic, while Chilean ambassador
to the United States, reflected this view, saying:[22]

Probably the single most important factor promoting the process
of modernization in the underdeveloped societies is precisely the
social pressure created by population growth. . . . What would
the effect be of reducing the social tensions due to population
growth, in the semi-feudal and oligarchical societies of so many
nations of the third world? Could it not be that a successful birth
control program carries with it the seeds of self-destruction for its
principal objective of modernization?

According to this logic, misery should be encouraged to
spread so that it will have to be cured.

For still others, especially those influenced by conservative
religious doctrine, children are an unmitigated blessing, and in
good time the economy will adjust to provide for all comers.
Argentina's President Ongañia expressed this view when he
said:[23]

The process of urbanization inherent in development promotes by
itself a gradual and spontaneous decrease in the number of children. And while this tendency is difficult to reverse, it can be

[21] J. Mayone Stycos, "Defusing the population bomb in Latin America,"
Congressional Record, February 9, 1967, A574.
[22] Ibid., A575.
[23] In his address to the meeting of ministers of public health of the Americas,
October, 1968.

modified with a policy of protection for the family, so that having children is not a burden but an advantage, for the spiritual satisfactions which they bring. The principal countries of Western Europe have reacted thus against decadent tendencies, which constitute a warning to countries which are still in a position to preserve their national vitality.

The trouble with this reasoning is that urbanization has no magic power to limit fertility. The birth rates of the more developed Western nations did decline as the countries modernized. But probably the greatest part of the decline in most of them was due to deliberate efforts by couples to restrict the number of their children because of the decreasing advantages and increasing disadvantages of having large families. Moreover, it must be noted that it took many years for the birth rates which accompanied industrialization and urbanization in nineteenth century Europe to decline. In the two nations with the fastest downward fertility trend, the Soviet Union and Japan, national abortion programs are often given credit for the declining birth rates; in both instances the major justification for the programs in the first place was to abolish the high rate of clandestine, dangerous abortions. Thus, to imply that urbanization will obviate the need for artificial birth prevention measures ignores the fact that reductions in births in urbanized countries are largely accomplished by just such measures.

The strong anti-U.S. reaction of Latin American nationalists, the tortured reasoning of some Latin American intellectuals, and the simplistic approaches of some leaders should not panic the United States into back-pedaling on its determination to help the Latin Americans cope with their population problem.

It is too early to assess the effect in Latin America of the papal encyclical, *On Human Life*, issued on July 29, 1968, which reaffirms the opposition of the Roman Catholic Church to artificial methods of contraception. The Pope called upon "rulers . . . who can do so much to safeguard moral customs," saying: "Do not allow the morality of your peoples to be degraded; do not permit that by legal means practices contrary to the natural and divine law be introduced into . . . the family. . . ." Some observers think that the Latin American governments will continue quietly to operate or tolerate family planning centers, leaving the moral debate to theologians and individual consciences.

Whether the Church will precipitate a battle with secular authorities over the issue of birth control in any Latin American country remains to be seen. Possibly some governments may abandon their support for birth control endeavors to avoid conflict with the hierarchy. While I would regret any setback to the incipient effort in Latin America to reduce the region's population growth, the Latin Americans themselves will be the judge of what course to follow.

What about the policy of the United States in view of the encyclical? Since Latin America is over 80 per cent Catholic, will the papal ruling render futile attempts to initiate birth control programs in the region? Should the United States abandon attempts to encourage a vigorous population policy in Latin America?

Consider the rates of population growth of the thirty-four predominantly Catholic countries in the world. Fifteen are increasing below the world's annual rate of 1.8 per cent. Twelve of these are in Europe, where 42.8 per cent of the world's Catholics live. For example, Spain (whose population is 99.7 per cent Catholic) has an annual rate of increase of only 0.8 per cent; Portugal (91.5 per cent Catholic) has a 0.7 per cent rate of increase; Austria (84.6 per cent Catholic) has a 0.5 per cent rate of increase. It is significant to note that all the Catholic countries of Europe have an annual rate of increase less than that of the United States (1.0 per cent). Looked at from another angle, among the forty-six slowest growth countries (those increasing at the world rate of 1.8 per cent or below over a five-year period), fifteen are predominantly Catholic.

Indications are there is no correlation between level of fertility and Catholicism. Predominantly Catholic countries outside the Western Hemisphere have achieved low birth rates, and there is evidence that Catholicism will not be an obstacle to family planning in Latin America.

In fact, very recent studies conducted among Catholic women in the major cities of Latin America indicate that a substantial and increasing number are using contraception. The average woman favors receiving birth control information and has practiced or will practice contraception before passing her childbearing years. Moreover, no consistent differences were found between Catholic and non-Catholic women in attitudes, contraceptive practices, or fertility. Further, the proportion of Catholic women who declared that they had tried to control their fertility rose with increasing levels of education.

Dr. Benjamin Viel of Chile has pointed out that in Santiago, among the wealthier families of strong Catholic persuasion, the birth rate is only 20 per 1,000, while among the lower class where "Catholicism exerts a doubtful influence . . . the birth rate, even with two abortions for every five births, reaches 40 per thousand." Dr. Viel concludes, "There can be no explanation for this other than that couples in the upper quarter use contraceptives that are unknown in the lower."[24]

Surveys in Rio de Janeiro, in Lima, and in Chimbote, Peru, are especially revealing. It was found that lower-class women are more sensitive than those of the upper classes to the economic disadvantages of additional children and desire fewer children, yet have the most. They are, apparently, ignorant of the modern contraceptive techniques with which the more privileged women are familiar.

Perhaps the most telling sign of the weakness of Church doctrine in influencing birth prevention in Latin America is

[24] *Latin America at the Crossroads,* Victor Fund for the International Planned Parenthood Federation, Report No. 3, September 1966, p. 21.

the alarming rate of induced abortion. No other Catholic stricture regarding interference with birth is as condemnatory as that which forbids terminating fetal life at any time after the moment of conception. Yet numerous studies and hospital experience in Latin America indicate a widespread disregard for Church teaching.

For example, a survey conducted in the Chilean cities of Santiago, Concepción, and Antofagasta in 1961 disclosed that just under one out of every four of 3,800 women aged twenty through forty-nine who were interviewed admitted having had at least one induced abortion. Of these, a quarter had had three or more abortions. A third of Santiago's induced abortions resulted in hospitalization.

In other Latin American countries where studies have been conducted, the record is equally abysmal. Intensive interviewing in Buenos Aires in clinics in Guillermo Rawson Hospital revealed that over 25 per cent of all pregnancies terminated in induced abortions. In the Caracas, Venezuela, maternity hospital Concepción Palaciao, there was one post-abortion hospital case for every four live births in 1964. Uruguay appears to hold the record, three induced abortions for every live birth recorded.

It must be noted that the startling abortion rates are not associated with pregnancies stemming from promiscuous relations. For example, in the Santiago study, 85 per cent of the induced abortions occurred among married women.

The high rate of induced abortion indicates that many Latin American women do wish to regulate the number of children they bear. Many, ignorant of modern contraceptive techniques, resort to primitive methods of contraception not condoned by the Catholic Church. When these fail, they take the most dangerous step to prevent birth—self-induced abortion.

One noted authority has summed up the situation in these words: "Every illegal abortion is one woman's desperate answer to her own personal over-population problem. In effect, it is her attempt to practice what we all advocate: responsible parenthood."[25]

As matters stand in Latin America (and so true of everywhere in the world), those least able must bear the burden of society's complacency and indifference—the poor and illiterate, especially neglected and abandoned children and those women burdened by too frequent pregnancies. In this circumstance it is questionable whether a better family life—a life of any kind—can be realized unless those able to are willing to pursue policy changes to meet the critical demands of twentieth century man.

Modern science and technology, emanating from the advanced countries, have sharply reduced mortality rates in Latin America, and few would argue that humanitarian developments should have been withheld from the people. But the introduction of life-saving drugs, new medical procedures, and sanitation into a region whose high birth rates have remained constant has created a population explosion and its accompanying economic and social problems.

As long as the Latin American governments wish to initiate and conduct birth control programs, the United States should be prepared to assist them, and withstand the protests of those in Latin America and elsewhere, who, for one reason or another, oppose birth control. Few innovations, domestic or foreign, do not have their detractors and opponents. In most cases, only governments can mount the necessary resources to deal with the population problem on the scale required.

Modern technology has developed a variety of contraceptive methods which could be helpful in controlling population growth. Birth prevention information and contraceptives do not have such obviously humane purposes as those measures which extend life. But no one who has examined the various implications of Latin America's population problem can dis-

[25] Dr. Mary S. Calderone, quoted in Thornburg, p. 30.

count the profoundly humanitarian aspects of checking the high rate of population growth which the region is experiencing.

There are, however, some caveats. First, birth control is not a substitute for economic development and social reform. It is an integral aspect of the total economic development process. Let me make clear that whatever is done in controlling population growth is only a part of a larger program which has as its goal the promotion of economic and social justice and human dignity. However, assistance for population programs in Latin America should be at least equal to all other assistance devoted to Alliance for Progress objectives.

Further, the only way the United States can evince its good faith in the delicate matter of birth control is to practice what we preach. The United States, with only 6 per cent of the world's population, is consuming between 35 and 40 per cent of the world's resources. We can hardly advocate a strong population policy for the developing countries while we continue a laissez-faire domestic policy with little concern about the demands our increasing population will make on the world's resources.

PART III

The Tools of Battle

7

Birth Control

THE JOYS of fatherhood and motherhood are among the most important experiences in life. Mankind has always wanted and cherished offspring; some of the saddest figures in history have been those to whom children have been denied.

Nothing can compare with the promise of a newborn child. Yet, if this promise is to be kept, this child needs all the love and care that a devoted mother and father can and must provide. We know that he needs more than the basic essentials of life; he needs a favorable material and psychological environment in the home, the community, and the larger world. Healthier, happier children growing up in a better environment will be better equipped emotionally and physically to face the changing, accelerating, highly competitive nation and the world of tomorrow.

If we are to build a better society, we must give closer attention to the needs of each newborn child. Surely we do not want to bring children into a world where deprivation of various kinds promises far too many of them little more than poverty, hunger, and despair. Whether we consider the "haves" or the "have-nots" among nations, no longer can we delude ourselves that the more children born, the better. We must give careful thought to the theories of other times: more hands to work the soil, more helpers to care for aging parents, more recruits to man armies, or more consumers to purchase the output of our private industries.

A new attitude toward birth challenges some of the beliefs and folklore of the past. In the long history of man, birth has always been one of the mysteries, bound up with hope, fear, superstition, pain, and joy—both a religious mystery and a mystery among natural phenomena. Man has long tried to fathom the unknowns of conception and birth. Through science we have learned much, and in the future through science we will learn even more amazing things about the unbelievably complex processes that are involved when a man and woman start a new life that will enter the world some 280 days later. Though the unknown is becoming known, many are still largely prisoners of the ignorance, taboos, and follies of the past.

Although practices to limit the conception and birth of children are ancient, birth control is a modern term, idea, and practice. Seemingly it could relate to a variety of measures to limit birth, or the number of births, whether by contraception, sterilization, abortion, or abstinence. As it is generally used, and as it is used in this book, birth control is broadly synonymous with contraception, and refers to a number of practices to prevent conception. Largely because the term contraception, and even the term birth control, connotes undesirable things to some people, a number of euphemisms, such as family planning, family limitation, child spacing, and planned parenthood, have come into use. Yet these terms also have their own meanings and usefulness. Family planning, for example, implies not only conscious decisions by husband and wife on how many children they shall have and when they shall have them, but also the making of such decisions as wisely as possible considering the many economic, social, and medical factors that bear on family well-being.

Parents thousands of years ago in ancient Rome, Greece,

and China discussed planning the size of a family by means of birth control. They were motivated, as many are motivated today, by a desire to have only those children who could be properly fed and cared for. Aristotle contended that civilization could be best served by limiting the number of children in a family. Though the idea of practicing birth control is thousands of years old, the biology of the role of the father in the creation of a human being was not firmly established until about three hundred years ago when the discovery of the microscope made it possible to see living human sperm. The father's role has, however, been the basic assumption behind many methods of birth control for a great many centuries.

Greek physicians and medical writers conducted research on contraceptive techniques centuries ago. Their discoveries were utilized by the Romans, but contrary to popular beliefs, knowledge of contraception was not diffused in the Roman world. It was not until the sixteenth century that a new advance in contraceptive technique was made. In 1564, an Italian anatomist, Gabriello Fallopio, recommended the use of a mechanical contraceptive. Mechanical contraceptives were employed during the eighteenth century both in England and on the Continent, but their use was primarily clandestine. As late as the eighteenth century contraceptives were still associated with immorality and vice. However, by the close of the nineteenth century this attitude was beginning to change. Although many were firmly opposed to contraception, a large number of informed people were aware of the concept, and public awareness created a climate for public debate and a change in attitude.

Thomas Malthus (1766–1834), a British curate, was the pioneer in modern thinking about the perils of overpopulation. The American and French revolutions and the industrial revolution already gathering steam in England seemed to offer hope that an era of increasing progress and prosperity for mankind was beginning. Malthus insisted that the progress which optimists were anticipating would be halted by the laws of nature. His concern that the human population would increase faster than the means of subsistence is stated in *An Essay on the Principles of Population as It Affects the Future Improvement of Society*. His line of reasoning was that the majority of the human race would be doomed to perpetual poverty and malnutrition. He felt that disease and war act as natural checks on population increase and so prevent a universal catastrophe. Malthus's first essay offered no alternative, but by 1803 his second edition included recommendations for "moral restraint."

Malthus's argument was that food supplies (subsistence) increased only in an arithmetic progression (2, 4, 6, 8, 10, 12, etc.), while population increased in a geometric progression (2, 4, 8, 16, 32, 64, etc.). He was saying that population would always tend to increase faster than the means of subsistence until halted by the inevitable checks of war, pestilence, or famine. Further, he went on to say that any improvement in man's capacities to produce, such as the steam engine and the power loom, would merely increase human misery by permitting a larger proportion of the population to exist in the same state of poverty as before the change was introduced. Malthus's essay began many years of controversy. Even today it is quoted in many discussions of the possibilities and problems of feeding the new millions of people born each year.

In 1822, Francis Place suggested that use of contraception was the answer to population problems—the moral restraint theory had a competitor. Place went beyond his public statement by distributing literature in which contraception was recommended to the working classes. This activity spread to the United States, where in 1831 Robert Owen published the first American booklet on birth control, "Moral Physiology." In 1832, Dr. Charles Knowlton, a Massachusetts physician, published a treatise on contraceptive methods entitled "Fruits of Philosophy." He eventually served a term in prison because of it. Increasingly, birth control became a subject of discussion in educated circles, but the great masses of people were still largely ignorant of contraception and the arguments for it.

In 1877, in England, the famous trial of Charles Bradlaugh and Annie Besant took place for their republishing of a version of Dr. Knowlton's "Fruits of Philosophy." This made contraception a hotly debated subject throughout Europe. Mrs. Besant used the interest as an opportunity to bring to the public's attention Malthus's essay on population. Bradlaugh and Mrs. Besant were both convicted, sentenced to six months imprisonment, and fined. However, they won an appeal on a technicality that the indictment did not contain the alleged obscene language. This trial resulted in a greater public awareness of the birth control issue. Circulation of the publication which the defendants were convicted for publishing increased tremendously.

The trial occurred at a time that favored the birth control movement, for industrialization and the fall of the death rate in Europe had resulted in a vastly increased population. The great depression of 1873 to 1896 led to widespread dislocation in agriculture and industry. Emancipation of women had begun, and many women were unwilling to bear the burden of unlimited childbearing. New legislation forbidding employment of children had reduced their value as income-earning assets. Education was made compulsory and this resulted in an increased financial burden on large families. Thus, the great economic and social changes that were in motion gave rise to a new interest in the concept of birth control.

Although the idea of contraception still did not receive general public acceptance, after 1878 there was little or no attempt to suppress birth control information by law in Europe. A number of books on birth control were published about this time. After World War I, social restrictions on dissemination of birth control information disappeared, and in 1921 the first birth control clinic was established in London by Marie Stopes.

In the United States, the birth control movement did not meet with such success. Dr. Knowlton's book was succeeded by other medical publications advancing the cause of birth control. Then, in 1873, birth control movements everywhere suffered a severe setback when, thanks to the efforts of Anthony Comstock, the United States Congress enacted a statute declaring contraceptives and contraceptive information obscene and excluded them from the mails. Shortly thereafter many states followed suit by passing statutes banning the sale and distribution of contraceptives. These laws were enforced with varying degrees of efficiency in different parts of the country, but, nevertheless, they hindered general acceptance of birth control in America.

No discussion of birth control and no historical review of the birth control movement anywhere in the world would be complete without giving special attention to the work of Mrs. Margaret Sanger, the courageous public health nurse who had the vision to understand the importance birth control programs would have in the modern world. She was one of the many so-called revolutionaries of the "Golden Age of American radicalism" in the early 1900's. Her work in the field of birth control began as a result of her experience in New York's Lower East Side immigrant slums, where, as in the slums of today, pregnancy was a chronic condition among poor women. In 1912, Mrs. Sanger had nursed back to life a Mrs. Sadie Sachs, who was hemorrhaging as a result of a self-induced abortion. After Mrs. Sachs at last recovered, she asked a doctor to tell her how to keep from becoming pregnant. His reply was, "Tell Jake to sleep on the roof." Mrs. Sanger was shocked by the plight of women like Mrs. Sachs, and she began to ask midwives, social workers, and doctors how poor people could limit their families. She found only ignorance and misunderstanding. Her friends continually warned her to keep off the subject of birth control or Anthony Comstock would bring his influence to bear on her.

While consulting the Library of Congress, the Boston Medical Library, and the New York Academy of Medicine, Mrs. Sanger learned that most of the information published on contraception was no better than the back-room chatter that could be heard in any city or town in America. Determined to find more practical information, she traveled to France where she found that women knew about contraception. After conferring with several authorities in Europe, she returned to America to begin her battle against Comstock, of whom it has been said that his "stunted neurotic nature and savage method of attack were responsible for the deplorable condition of a whole generation of women left physically damaged and spiritually crippled from the results of abortion."

In his book, *The Birth Controllers*, Peter Fryer sums up the man and the law that contributed most to suppressing the concept of birth control in the United States and elsewhere:

Anthony Comstock (1844-1915), originator of the law in question, was a Civil War veteran, dry-goods salesman, and sex-obsessed blue nose, who as Chief Special Agent for the New York Society for the Supression of Vice, was responsible for the arrest of 3,873 persons, of whom 2,911 were convicted. His notorious section, 211 of the Federal Criminal Code, provided a maximum penalty of five years' imprisonment and a fine of $5,000 for anyone who sent through the mails any paper, writing, or advertisement or a representation that any article, instrument, substance, drug, medicine, or thing made, or can be, used or applied, for preventing conception, or any description calculated to induce or incite a person to so use or apply any such article, instrument, substance, drug, medicine, or thing. When the first draft of this section went before Congress it contained the following exemptions: except from a physician in good standing, given in good faith. Why this exemption was later omitted is a mystery. The bill went through without any debate until after it was passed; even then, only one speech was made in its favor, and that speech (by Representative Merriam of Locust Grove, New York) was never spoken in the House but printed, by leave, in the Congressional Record. Comstock afterwards claimed that he simply showed specimens of disgusting pictures and publications to members of Congress, which so incensed them that the bill went through. Interviewed for *Harper's Weekly* just before his death, Comstock was asked why he classed contraceptives with pornographic objects, since European scientists who advocated their use had no desire to debauch children. He replied, after an impatient reference to theorizers who did not know human nature, "If you open the door to anything, the filth will all pour in and the degradation of youth will follow!"

This was the man and the law that confronted Mrs. Sanger when she returned to the United States from Europe, filled with ideas about a movement to provide information and education to the women who desired to limit and plan their families. In 1914 she began to make public speeches on the subject and published a monthly magazine, *The Woman Rebel*. Soon after, she was arrested and indicted under the Comstock law. Not having enough time to prepare for her defense, she fled to Europe. While she was out of the country her husband was tricked into sending a birth control pamphlet to Mr. Comstock and was promptly imprisoned for a short time. The publication that he sent to Comstock was a copy of Mrs. Sanger's pamphlet, "Family Limitation." This classic publication on birth control in America was a typical example of the practical and common-sense manner in which Mrs. Sanger approached the subject of family limitation. Her logical and sincere discussion of birth control in the pamphlet is just as applicable today to the needs of women throughout the world as it was in 1914 when the pamphlet was first published.

Mrs. Sanger stated the question of birth control frankly in the introduction to "Family Limitation":

There is no need for anyone to explain to the working men and women in America what this pamphlet is written for or why it is necessary that they should have this information. They know better than I could tell them, so I shall not try. . . .

Women of the working class, especially wageworkers, should not have more than two children at most. The average working man can support no more and the average woman can take care of no more in decent fashion.

She ended the introduction with this appeal: "Spread this important knowledge!" For half a century she did just that.

Mrs. Sanger returned to the United States in 1916, and opened, in Brooklyn, New York, the first birth control clinic in the United States. As might have been expected, the clinic was soon raided and closed by the police, and Mrs. Sanger and one of her sisters (Mrs. Sanger was one of eleven children) were both sentenced to jail in 1917. Undaunted by harassment, they founded the National Birth Control League later that year.

With varying degrees of success, Mrs. Sanger continued her efforts to repeal or amend the restrictive federal law on birth control. One of the most influential associations she developed was with progressive American physicians. Mrs. Sanger's continued effort paid off in 1925, when the Obstetrics and Gynecological Advisory Division of the American Medical Association passed a resolution recommending changing the laws to allow physicians to give contraceptive advice. Her efforts and the statements of the AMA did much to alleviate the general opposition to birth control in America. Public reaction against the concept of birth control began to ease significantly, and other breakthroughs began to occur rapidly. In 1929 another New York birth control clinic was raided and its directors arrested under the Comstock law. Later they were discharged, and the clinic continued to take patients. Thus, these developments greatly reduced the Comstock law's ability to suppress information on contraception, and essentially marked the beginning of the end of effective opposition to birth control in the United States.

In 1931, the Federal Council of the Churches of Christ

published a report favoring birth control. This was another landmark in the crusade of Mrs. Sanger and others who were interested in making birth control services available to those Americans who needed and wanted them. Enforcement of the Comstock law was on its last legs. In 1936, enforcement was further relaxed when the Circuit Court of Appeals, Second Circuit, reversed a ruling in the District Court and held that "contraceptives imported for a lawful purpose did not come within the restrictions of the federal law." Finally in 1937, the first phase of Margaret Sanger's crusade for the birth control movement was rewarded when the American Medical Association unanimously agreed to accept birth control "as an integral part of medical practice and education" in America.

So it was that the one-woman crusade of 1914 became nationally accepted by American medicine in 1937. Yet Mrs. Sanger did not stop there, for she began to lecture in Japan and China and elsewhere in the world about the need for birth control in our modern society. She did much to influence the formation of scientific organizations on population problems. She was the founder and, until her death in 1966, the president emeritus of the International Planned Parenthood Federation.

Margaret Sanger campaigned on behalf of birth control for over fifty years. She stands out today as one of the great Americans of this or any other century; great in the sense of the depth of her vision, the creativity of the programs she instituted, and the generosity with which she gave mankind her knowledge and purpose toward a just and righteous cause.

It wasn't until *1965* that the Supreme Court handed down the decision that once and for all struck down the archaic Comstock law. The historic and landmark case I refer to is *Griswold* v. *Connecticut*. This case tested the toughest Comstock law in America, Connecticut's 1879 statute which made the use of any drug, medical article, or instrument to prevent conception an offense punishable by a fine and up to a year in prison. It further stated that anyone who "assists, abets, counsels, causes, hires, or commands another to commit any offense" could be similarly prosecuted. Justice William O. Douglas, writing the majority opinion for the Supreme Court, declared that the case concerned "a relationship lying within the zone of privacy created by several fundamental constitutional guarantees" and said that Connecticut law "in forbidding the use of contraceptives rather than regulating their manufacture or sale, seeks to achieve its goals by means having a maximum destructive impact upon that relationship. We deal with the right of privacy older than the Bill of Rights—older than our political parties, older than our school system." He added, "Marriage is a coming together for a better or worse, hopefully enduring and intimate to the degree of being sacred." The two dissenting justices, Potter Stewart and Hugo Black, both believed that the Connecticut law was offensive, but constitutional. The Supreme Court decision set off a chain reaction across the country; those states with Comstock laws began to remove all restrictions on the dissemination of birth control information and to permit the sale of contraceptives to everyone over the age of sixteen.[1]

Of course, the revolutionary changes that have taken place in attitudes and practices relating to birth control did not take place in a vacuum. Beginning with World War I and continuing through the end of World War II, there began to be a rapidly widening gap between birth and death rates, and some demographers began to term our population increases a population explosion. Whereas the world's population had been growing about 10 million a year before World War II, it is now increasing at an annual rate of 25 million or more per year. Without the world realizing it, time was moving on, and the years were growing short when famine would become a

[1] U.S. Congress, Senate, Committee on Government Operations, subcommittee on Foreign Aid Expenditures, *Hearings,* 89th Cong. 2d sess., 1965, p. 1271.

reality. During all this time India, China, and other parts of Asia, Latin America, and even the United States began to feel the pressures of population increases. To learned observers it looked very much as if the gloomy prediction of Malthus would sooner or later be fulfilled.

Social scientists and other leaders in the United States and other countries were trying to alert the public to the looming threat of runaway population growth rates. But such men as Fairfield Osborne, then president of the New York Zoological Society; William Vogt, then national director of the Planned Parenthood Association; and Robert C. Cook, past president of the Population Reference Bureau, were criticized by some experts for pointing out that population growth was indeed outracing the food supply. They were labeled neo-Malthusians and charged with attempting to scare the world by reviving a long disapproved doctrine of Malthus. Their critics failed to realize these men differed from Malthus in that they did not believe it was necessary to wait for disasters of war, famine, or pestilence to occur in order to control population. They wanted to see the population explosion arrested through responsible, voluntary limitation of human fertility.

In 1959, a study commission, headed by General William H. Draper (recently national chairman of the Population Crises Committee), was formed to review the United States foreign aid program under which we had been spending up to $5 billion annually to help underdeveloped nations improve their economies and raise the standard of living of their people. The commission found that, in country after country, the value of our foreign aid was being wiped out by high rates of population growth. Instead of per-capita incomes increasing they remained at low levels and in some countries actually were declining.

Despite the commission's findings, for the past decade we have yet to alter our foreign policy priorities sufficiently to help alleviate growing food and population problems. The Draper commission was not merely content to assemble a set of statistics; it boldly recommended to President Eisenhower that the United States help countries that requested our aid "in the formulation of their plans designed to deal with the problem of rapid population growth." The commission's report promoted a great debate in the press and over television concerning both population problems and birth control. Many who had never spoken out before did so in support of the commission's recommendations. However, the Catholic bishops of the United States announced that they would oppose any public program to promote birth control at home or abroad. When President Eisenhower was questioned about the Draper report at a press conference, he discouraged further action by declaring, "I cannot imagine anything more emphatically a subject that is not a proper political or governmental activity or function or responsibility. . . . This government has not, and will not as long as I am here, have a program that has to do with birth control. That's not our business."

Ironically, it was a Catholic President who took the first real step forward in establishing a national policy on population and family planning programs. In December, 1962, President Kennedy signaled the beginning of a policy change at the federal level when he authorized our United Nations delegation to support a UN proposal to permit the World Health Organization to provide birth control assistance to countries requesting it. A year later, former President Eisenhower reversed his stand when he wrote in a magazine article:

I opposed the use of federal funds to provide birth control information to countries we are aiding because I felt this would violate the deepest religious convictions of large groups of taxpayers. As I now look back it may be that I was carrying that conviction too far. . . . The time has come when we must take into account the effect of the population explosion on our mutual assistance program. A large proportion of this increase is occurring in countries who are having difficulty in feeding and clothing their present population and desperately need a little elbowroom while they improve their resources. . . . There is no real progress or security to a nation which, with outside help, raises its productive capacities by two percent a year while the population rises by three percent. . . . I want to stress the responsibility we have for finding some realistic means in containing this human explosion.

In 1963, another major step was taken to change our national policy when the Congress passed and President Kennedy signed the first foreign aid bill that included a funding authorization for population studies. That year the United States granted $500,000 to the World Health Organization in support of population research. In 1965 President Johnson's now famous State of the Union message marked a new era of U.S. involvement in population and family planning programs.

In 1965 and 1966 the President and the Congress placed increased emphasis on our involvement in population matters, both domestic and foreign. But despite the effort by Senators Ernest Gruening, Joseph Clark, and others to get the domestic bureaucracy more deeply involved in this field, there was still great reluctance to commit funds in this vitally important area.

The Office of Economic Opportunity (OEO) was the first federal agency to establish an effective pattern of support for family planning programs—in this case the funding of grassroots community organizations. However, the Department of Health, Education, and Welfare is the organization with the potential to administer the kind of national population and family planning program equal to U.S. needs. I have introduced legislation in the 91st Congress that I believe will improve U.S. assistance in this field.

There are several different departments, agencies, and bureaus engaged in promoting family planning services in the U.S., and perhaps this is one of the reasons why, despite millions of dollars allocated, the assistance reaches less than 25 per cent of those women who need and want it.*

Presently the Agency for International Development is administering a $50-million-dollar program. The Department of Health, Education, and Welfare spent roughly $28 million on family planning programs during fiscal 1967–68; the Food and Drug Administration evaluates the safety of contraceptives, regulates labeling and other aspects of the distribution of such products; and the Office of Education provides funds in support of educational programs in family life and sex education. The last of these perhaps is one of the key areas where so much could be done to improve attitudes and increase awareness of the importance of responsible parenthood.

The National Institutes of Child Health and Human Development conducts and supports clinical, biomedical, and behavioral research in family planning, birth control, and population. The Public Health Service assists state and local governments in making family planning information and services available and provides training for public health service personnel in family planning and related subjects.

The Department of the Interior also provides family planning assistance, making birth control information and services available to American Indians on government reservations; to Indians, Eskimos, and Aleuts in Alaska; and to natives of the Pacific Island Trust Territories. Most recently legislation has been passed to amend the 1967 Social Security Amendments, authorizing funds for family planning services to be provided to families with dependent children. Also payments for family planning services are available under Medicaid. Through funds administered by the Department of Health, Education, and Welfare's Children's Bureau, legislation passed earmarks

* Author's note: A review of U.S. government assistance from 1962–1967 can be found in the *Hearings on S. 1676* of the Subcommittee on Foreign Aid Expenditures, Committee on Government Operations, U.S. Senate, 90th Congress, 2d session.

6 per cent of all funds appropriated for maternal and child health services for family planning services.

Thus, in the comparatively few years since Anthony Comstock's repressive influence ruled the land and since Margaret Sanger's heart bled over the plight of a poor Lower East Side housewife, the federal government has established programs in family planning and population studies. Yet, there are uninformed Sadie Sachses in the United States and all over the world, and we have only made a beginning in the vast set of programs needed to "spread this important knowledge." As a matter of fact, we need to gain even more knowledge and to spread that also. Some of the most interesting research being done today is in the area of birth control. Without a doubt, the foremost reason that birth control has been practiced so little in past decades and centuries has been the woeful lag in the discovery of efficient, effective, readily acceptable contraceptive techniques. Indeed, until recently, our best knowledge in this field was little better than man's knowledge of transportation before someone invented the wheel. Methods passed along from generation to generation by folklore were so unsatisfactory and ineffective there is little wonder the Sadie Sachses of the world lost hope.

More recently the transitional methods, such as those advocated by Margaret Sanger, left much to be desired in effectiveness, convenience, and acceptability. All such approaches to contraception are now largely being relegated to the past, in favor of two modern birth control methods: oral contraceptives (the pill) and intra-uterine devices (such as the loop). There is, of course, still another kind of birth control: that obtained through the surgical sterilization of men or women. Though it is usually irreversible, it has gained acceptance and popularity in some areas. During the late 1950's, in the United States, it is estimated there were 110,000 voluntary sterilizations annually.

By the middle of 1967, the recently discovered oral contraceptives had gained such popularity that 6.5 million women in

the United States were estimated to be "on the pill." An equal
number of women in other countries were believed to be
taking oral contraceptives. Although the pill is more commonly used in Australia, New Zealand, Canada, the United
Kingdom, and the Scandinavian countries, more than 2 million women in Latin America are said to be taking the pill. In
this country, it is most popular among younger women who
have better-than-average education, but it is widely believed
that nearly all women, even those with limited education, can
be instructed to take the pill with reasonable consistency. The
pill has evidently been more acceptable than other methods of
contraception, and is believed to have greater potential in the
developing countries than the intra-uterine devices (IUD).

There are two types of oral contraceptives now in general
use. One type consists of identical tablets containing progestin
and estrogen and the other type consists of some tablets
containing estrogen and others containing progestin and
estrogen. The pills suppress ovulation, and studies indicate
that they are almost completely effective in preventing unwanted pregnancy when taken according to directions. Undesirable side effects have been experienced by some women
taking the pill, and some of these side effects are serious.
There is an *urgent* need for continued study of the effects of
the pill and for continued research for a better, safer contraceptive.

Modern intra-uterine contraceptive devices, such as the
loop, are small objects made of chemically inert materials,
such as plastic and stainless steel, that are inserted in the uterus
to remain there indefinitely. The IUD is suitable for use in
large-scale birth control programs. For most couples, it is
effective, safe, and acceptable. Generally, once the IUD is
inserted—and assuming it remains in place—no further attention is needed. It is believed that up to 2 million women in the
United States and about 5 million women in the world are
using IUD's. These have been in widespread use in national
family planning programs, especially in Asia. One disadvan-

tage of an IUD is that when inserted it may become displaced without the knowledge of the wearer. Also, some women suffer undesirable side effects from the use of IUD's. Research continues in order to find a more suitable IUD.

New research on contraception is resulting in exciting discoveries that promise to provide a more acceptable, convenient, economical, and effective method than the pill or IUD. In the future a woman may receive an injection that will prevent pregnancy for an extended time, perhaps even as long as she wishes. There may also be a pill for men, or an injection that will render them sterile for an extended time or as long as they wish. Undoubtedly, improvements will be made in the existing pill, and perhaps a woman may have to take only one pill a month, or even one pill a year, to prevent pregnancy. It is entirely possible that substances will be discovered that, when implanted under the skin of a man or woman, will serve as a contraceptive for weeks or months. Researchers even speak of the possibility of a progestin that could be absorbed by a woman through her skin, perhaps from a ring or from a cosmetic, and prevent pregnancy for an indefinite time. Just as it is now possible to inoculate a person against a disease, it may become possible to inoculate a woman so that she will be immune to fertilization. All of these possibilities and many more are, and will continue to be, the subject of research. While some of the possibilities that have been suggested may seem highly speculative, the discoveries that actually will be made in coming years are likely to be even more amazing. We will have even more useful knowledge to spread. The problem arises in the determination and resolve to make wise use of this knowledge.

8

The Green Revolution

EFFECTIVE research in tropical agriculture is an essential weapon in the battle to avert famine, chaos, and political and social unrest in the world. It may come as a surprise to many, but there is no large-scale tropical agricultural research being conducted now, and there will be none for many years unless we change our foreign policy drastically to give improved agricultural production a major priority.

Although both the executive and legislative branches of government have stated their concern, the funds appropriated for this particular area are far below required levels. Here in America, we have learned to grow temperate-zone crops such as wheat, corn, potatoes, and other foodstuffs in such abundance we subsidize farmers to limit their production. Much of our country has a good climate and soils excellent for farming. Also, our farm technology has made us one of the leaders in the world in yields per acre. Unfortunately, most of the developing countries have not had such success. Despite the so-called green revolution or agricultural revolution hailed by so many observers, millions of people in Asia, Africa, and Latin America live on a daily subsistence basis. There, the nutritional levels are very low—usually below the minimum daily caloric level considered necessary for health—and there are several reasons for this. In addition to the ever-present continuing high population growth rates, some of the developing nations of the world have a poor system of land ownership, and land tenure reforms are slow to be accepted, cumbersome to establish, and expensive to implement. Large feudal land holdings stifle incentive and act to limit improvement in agricultural production, but fortunately, some national leaders recognize the importance of land reform as it relates to farm production and over-all economic growth.

Lack of technical assistance to farmers also limits the expansion of agriculture production. Research, teaching, and extension experts skilled in plant breeding, fertilizers, cultivation, irrigation, and other aspects of agriculture are in short supply or nonexistent in many areas on all levels.

Nation-builders, although recognizing the need for greater emphasis on agricultural production, have failed to establish long-range plans and firm commitments of funds for expanding agricultural production in the tropics.

Among the most frightening aspects of the man-land-food equation are the ominous implications of the relationship between malnutrition and mental growth. There is substantial evidence to suggest a correlation between mental retardation and malnutrition in the early years of a child's development. The contention is that the damage to a child's mental development due to childhood malnutrition may be irreversible (some authorities contend this has never been scientifically proved) and may have serious implications on the national development of a particular country.[1] If a child's full mental and physical capacities are retarded, then that individual's future capacity to contribute to society will be limited.

Former Secretary of Defense Robert McNamara, in his first

[1] Allen D. Berg, "Malnutrition and National Development," *Foreign Affairs* October, 1967.

major address as the new president of the World Bank, emphasized that in the next five-year program the most important area of World Bank activity, other than population assistance, would be aid to agriculture. "Agricultural assistance," he said, "is one that gives us a breathing spell in the race between man and his resources." And the eminent statesman and philosopher, C. P. Snow, stated recently that world developments have given him very little reason to hope that the richer countries will ever co-operate with each other sufficiently to head off a collision between soaring population and a limited world food supply, with staggering famine the result. He also stated, "Most informed opinion believe that the collision is going to take place. At best this will mean local famines to begin with, at worst the local famines will spread into a *sea of hunger*. The usual date predicted for the beginning of the local famine is 1975 to 1980." The late Dr. Max Millikan, director of the Center for International Studies of the Massachusetts Institute of Technology, stated before the House Committee on Agriculture: "Every effort must clearly be expended to reduce this [world] population growth as rapidly as possible if we are to avoid mass starvation in the coming century."

The problem is truly immense in scope and has significance transcending political and social ideologies and geographic boundaries. There is no escape for man from the food shortages that confront entire continents. There is no easy way for the "affluent society" to look the other way and decide that the problem is not theirs—just a nasty subject with no relevance to their everyday problems. The time has now come for America to examine its foreign policy priorities with due consideration to the predictions of imminent world-wide food shortages that are impossible to separate from the issue of international peace and security.

The more advanced, fully industrialized countries enjoy an ample supply of food. As in our own country, however, distribution of available food still remains a serious problem. An even more critical problem in the underdeveloped regions of Asia, Africa, and Latin America is the *production* of food. In 1967 there was an increase of nearly 5 per cent. This largest single-year increase since 1953 followed two years of discouraging results; agricultural production in 1965 and 1966 was at a low level because of adverse weather and continuing deficiencies in farming. In 1967 favorable weather coincided with a payoff in long-term adaptive agricultural research and development efforts in most of the underdeveloped countries to produce good cereal crops, particularly in the Far East, Africa, and Latin America. The index of food production in these regions rose by 6.7 per cent, 6.1 per cent, and 5 per cent respectively. In the Near East production increased about 4 per cent.

The food production figures, when considered alone, seem to support optimistic predictions of advances in the war on hunger. However, examination of the indices of total food production, population growth, and per-capita food production for the three underdeveloped regions for the period 1952 through 1967 shows that the total food production increases have averaged only 3.8 per cent per year. Meanwhile population increases have averaged 2.8 per cent per year and the result has been an average gain in per-capita food production of *only seven-tenths of one per cent per year*. What is worse, for a fifteen-year period gains in per-capita food production in the underdeveloped regions exceeded 1 per cent in only five years (1953, 1955, 1956, 1958, and 1967). These statistics and the assessments exclude mainland China.[2] Average annual gain in per-capita food production during the years 1952 through 1959 was 1.3 per cent, and gains during the years 1960 through 1967 were so slight as to leave the index for 1967 unchanged from that of 1960 in the underdeveloped

[2] UN/FAO, *Monthly Bulletin of Agricultural Economics and Statistics,* Volume 17, July-August, 1968, pp. 16, 17.

countries. By comparison, per-capita food production in the developed regions of the world (North America, Europe, the USSR, and Oceania) increased an average of 1.8 per cent per year over the fifteen-year period; increases averaged 1.8 per cent during the years 1960 through 1967. During the fifteen-year period total food production increased at an average annual rate of 3.4 per cent and the population growth rate, which averaged about 1.4 per cent, was generally declining.[3]

In spite of the encouraging gains of 1967, the continued expansion of population in underdeveloped areas of the world has almost, if not completely, negated any gains made in total food output. Keep in mind, however, that gains during the fifteen years, 1952 through 1967, were in the early half of that period.

My attempts to project demand for food must rely largely on value judgments not supported by available data. However, the Economic Research Service of the U.S. Department of Agriculture in 1964 formulated a "world food balance" on the basis of estimates of food requirements for the world in 1970.[4] Such forecasts are of necessity based on a set of assumptions, such as a continuation of population growth rates, political stability, absence of natural catastrophes, continued economic development, continued real per-capita income growth, and relative stability in price relationships among products within countries on a round-the-world basis. Using the reference standards for nutritional levels developed by the UN Food and Agriculture Organization, the Economic Research Service calculated the size of the 1970 "gap" in terms of the food sources of calories, protein, and fat.

According to these calculations, by 1970 some *54 million tons* of food grains will be needed to close the food gap according to *calorie* needs. For *protein* needs in the under-

[3] Ibid.
[4] USDA Economic Research Service, *The World Food Budget, 1970,* Foreign Agriculture Economic Report No. 19, Washington, October, 1964.

developed regions, from 6 to 13 million tons of food will be required, depending on the sources used, i.e., 6.5 million tons of non-fat dry milk or 3 million tons of fish protein concentrates (for animal protein deficits) plus 6.7 million tons of dry beans and peas or 3.2 million tons of soy grits (for plant protein deficits). For needed *fats*, 3.1 million tons of vegetable oils will be needed.

If the United States should be able to export a sufficient amount of food to meet these projected requirements, what would this all mean in terms of dollars? Based upon 1963 U.S. export prices, the cost of meeting these fantastic needs is estimated at from $6.7 to $7.5 billion annually, depending upon the choice of protein foods.[5] If the calculations exclude Communist Asia and if they are based on using the cheaper protein foods, the estimated cost of meeting the nutritional needs of underdeveloped areas of 1970 would be reduced to about $2.5 billion. Most ($2.1 billion) of this cost would be needed to meet needs in free-world Asian nations, of which $872 million would be accounted for by India's annual needs alone. To me, these costs and these food estimates are incredible—the tremendous food production deficits in the world and the unprecedented, widespread, rapid acceleration in population growth rates are not only perpetuating "have-not" nations; they are creating a "have-not" world!

What, then, is America doing to improve the food production capacities of the developing world? What additional funds are being allocated to improve the ability of the have-not world to feed itself? Despite all the evidence that suggests we should be allocating more money for this most worthwhile endeavor, America is actually providing less money now than in the past. On October 10, 1968, House and Senate conferees agreed on a fiscal 1969 foreign aid appropriations bill. AID officials had asked for about $800 million for agricultural assistance, but because of the appropriations cuts, AID officials

[5] Ibid.

estimated that expenditures for this work would have to be reduced to about $435 million. This compares with $569 million for agricultural aid in the fiscal year ended June 30, 1968. Thus the evidence of today's large-scale world food needs has not changed the attitude of the American public and the U.S. Congress toward greater American involvement in self-help agriculture production programs.

The problems of our inner cities and the war in Vietnam have resulted in a feeling that perhaps we Americans cannot solve the problems of the world and we had better concentrate on care of our own citizens. I agree that we should do more for our citizens. However, the realities of international politics dictate that the troubles the developing countries have should be of concern to us. For America's future is tied directly to the future of the developing countries of the world. Therefore, the problems they face demand our resolve to help them. To this end we should expand our agricultural research knowledge at home and enable our universities to send technical advisers overseas and to train more U.S. and foreign students in agricultural development—particularly tropical agriculture development.

A report prepared by a world food supply panel of the President's Science Advisory Committee was made available to the public in May, 1967. On the basis of demographic and nutritional analyses, it states that food production in the underdeveloped countries must approximately double in the period 1965 to 1985 "if the critical physiological needs of rapidly expanding populations are to be met." Within ten to fifteen years, when food shortages become even more critical, it may be too late to provide workable solutions. The conclusions of the panel were:

1. "The scale, superiority, and duration of the world food problem is so great that a massive, long-range, innovative effort unprecedented in human history will be required to master it." I would add here that although the panel was speaking about food problems specifically, this recommenda-

tion certainly relates to the magnitude of effort required to master the population problem also.

2. "The solution of the problem, which would exist after about 1985, demands that programs of population control be initiated now. For the immediate future, the food supply is critical."

3. "The food supply is directly related to agriculture development and, in turn, agriculture development and overall economic development are critically interdependent in hungry countries." I would also say that food supply is also directly related to international peace and security.

4. "A strategy for attacking the world food problem will, of necessity, encompass the entire foreign economic assistance of the U.S. in cooperation with other developed countries, voluntary institutions, and international organizations."

The world food supply panel considered all possible food sources, including both unexploited products and unexplored methods, in estimating the food required to meet present shortages and provide for population growth in the future. Among the sources considered were new foods from the sea, certain types of bacteria, petroleum, and synthetics. The panel's conclusion was that there is "no panacea to this global problem." Even if the marine resources that promise to provide additional food throughout the world were increased to twenty times the amount of food we derive from the sea at present, it is estimated that this would still have no major impact on the world food problem.

It is important to understand that, although no one source of food supply offers a panacea, research must be continued on all fronts if we expect to achieve some semblance of a balance between food and population in the near future. Agricultural assistance must be focused on increasing the proper use of fertilizers, pesticides, new varieties of plants, appropriate machinery, and available water supplies. But improved farm technology must also be co-ordinated with additional attention by local governments to improve transportation, marketing systems, price supports, food preservation, and, most important of all, to provide the farmer with incentives to increase his production.

The question of whether the job can be done is answered easily enough. The success of the National Aeronautics and Space Administration in landing a man on the moon in a decade proves that America can marshal the necessary scientific and technical expertise to accomplish herculean tasks. The problem of hunger in today's world is huge and it is getting bigger every day. The real question is, *do we want to help avert famine?* Do we want to devote unselfishly a large amount of funds and manpower to help virtually half the world population? The pessimistic view of our domestic problems suggests that the American democratic experiment is now being severely tested. If America is to survive, our national priorities must be geared to the tasks facing us. Public and private technical and capital assistance in agriculture must be a number one priority in the minds of the American public.

If we do not develop the kind of grand strategy that the presidential panel concluded would be necessary to solve the food shortage problem, population growth among the underdeveloped nations will pass the point of no return, and political stability and social unrest will compound the problems of malnutrition and economic deterioration to the point where no reasonable solution can be found. On the other hand, if a massive and unprecedented effort is mounted, if population growth rates are brought under control, and if food production is improved in the tropics and subtropics, a balance between food supply and population will become a reality.

The problems of the less developed nations defy uncomplicated solutions comparable to the Point Four Program of the 1940's. Those countries requiring assistance after World War II were developed, industrialized nations that had the technical knowledge to rebuild but lacked capital. Today the task of providing economic assistance to developing countries is more complex, requiring a comprehensive approach toward the nation-building concept. Countries needing foreign economic assistance today are still largely dependent on agriculture and have very little technical expertise. The "gap" that we often read about in reference to have-not nations is the technical knowledge gap. Without capital for public enterprises such as schools, a nation fails to improve its educational base, and therefore its capacity to move toward a technical industrialized society.

The ever-increasing food requirements of exploding populations further frustrate efforts to achieve economic growth. Funds that should be used for education, health, and agricultural improvement are drained by food import costs. Food shipments to prevent hunger and starvation can certainly be justified when natural disasters, such as flooding or drought, limit normal production of crops. However, I do not believe we should encourage long-term food aid programs without also requiring self-help improvement of agricultural production within a recipient country. Contrary to the belief of some that improvement of agricultural production capacities of a developing country will hurt our food export programs, the fact is that improved agricultural production in the tropical and subtropical areas of the world will have the effect of improving our world-wide trade relationships and, ironically enough, improve our own export sales of food substantially.

The study panel on world food supply estimated that there is available for cultivation and crop growing approximately twice the amount of potentially arable land than previously estimated. Unfortunately, lack of funds and expert direction on how to properly clear, drain, or irrigate the land and prepare it for crop production will probably prevent this additional land from being used in the critical years before the end of the twentieth century. This means that we must at once give particular attention to increasing the productivity of the available land suitable for cultivation, and at the same time begin to assist in establishing institutional agriculture research capability in the developing countries.

Most of the developing countries are in or near the tropics. One exception in Latin America is Uruguay, which lies entirely within the temperate zone. In North Africa, only Morocco and Tunisia are entirely within the temperate zone.

A common misconception among development assistance administrators is that the temperate-zone crops can be easily adapted to tropical areas. This is not true. Experts now know that adaptive tropical agricultural research is needed as a basis for working with temperate-zone crops in tropical zones. Also needed is tropical agriculture research *in* the country concerned. For adaptive research is only a portion of the researcher's tool. He must do research on crops typical of the area—as well as adaptive research on crops grown in other climates. H. David Thurston of Cornell University recently wrote that "agriculture research in tropical areas in the past has been primarily on cash and plantation crops, while food crops—the plants that people eat, especially in the hot humid tropics—have been largely ignored by research workers."

Such crops as cassava, yams, and coconut are potentially almost equal to rice and maize in rank and importance as principal food production sources in the tropics. Plantains (cooking bananas) and legumes (beans, peas, chickpeas, etc.) constitute other major food sources in tropical countries. Yields of cassava in Brazil, expressed as calories per hectare, are about three times those from corn or rice. The starchy root and tuber crops (such as cassava) and plantains have a real potential for rapidly reducing food shortages in tropical countries. To the development assistance administrator, the researcher in agriculture, and the foreign policy maker, the words cassava and plantain should become as well known and common as wheat, corn, and rice.

Cassava is known in different countries by a variety of names, including manioc, manihot, and yuca. It is one of the most important of the tropical root crops native to Central and South America and is now cultivated in nearly all tropical areas, including West Africa and Malaysia. The edible portion of the plant is a large tuber, containing hydrocyanic acid which must be neutralized before the tuber can be used for food. This may be accomplished by sun-drying the roots and then pounding them into a coarse meal. Another method involves machine preparation in which roots are shredded into a pulp, then washed and dried. The yield is a powdery starch, known in its commercial form as tapioca. The meal is prepared in a variety of ways, usually it is eaten as a porridge or spoon bread. It is low in protein, but high in caloric content.

According to FAO statistics, some 9 million hectares (22.2 million acres) yielded 77.6 metric tons of cassava throughout the world in 1966. Production centered in the underdeveloped, tropical regions; the largest producers were Latin America (29.9 million metric tons) and the Far East (18.2 million metric tons). The acreage devoted to cassava was reported at nearly 6 million acres in Latin America, 11.3 million acres in Africa, and 5.7 million acres in the Far East.

This food crop is virtually ignored by agricultural researchers. In the January, 1969, issue of *Bioscience* there is an article by H. David Thurston entitled "Tropical Agriculture—A Key to the World Food Crisis." In that article Thurston refers to a professional journal, *The Review of Applied Mycology* (R.A.M.), probably the best journal for information on plant diseases throughout the world. He states: "From 1945 to 1965 there were 119 references to cassava in the R.A.M., or six references per year. Carnations were on the same page and I noted 350 references during the same period or 17 references per year. In 1966, the R.A.M. had two references to cassava diseases and 17 to carnation diseases. These figures illustrate how agriculture research (on a worldwide basis) is not giving some of the important food crops in the tropics the attention they need." I am not implying that research on carnations is not valuable. However, Thurston's comparison of the amount of plant disease research on carnations and the amount on cassava seems to support the position that research on basic tropical food crops is insignificant in comparison to other relatively unimportant plants.

One of the arguments that nutritionists give for avoiding concentrated research on the production of crops such as cassava and yams is that they are primarily made up of carbohydrates and have a low protein content. Yet some experts state that there are varieties of such crops with an appreciable protein content and that much might be done in a breeding program to increase it.

Since the war, AID, universities, private foundations, FAO, and the OAS have done a considerable amount of agricultural research in the tropics, but unfortunately there is still not enough emphasis in comparison to the need.

Billions of dollars have been spent over the years for temperate-zone agricultural research in the United States. We enjoy a farming technology and yields per acre the likes of which are unknown to the rest of the world. Farmers, students, and scientists from all over the world come to observe our farms, our great corn and wheat belts, our state agricultural colleges, experiment stations, and extension services; in comparison, success stories about agricultural research in the tropics are extremely hard to find.

One of the outstanding exceptions to this is the development of the miracle rice IR–8 and IR–5 by the International Rice Research Institute, in Los Baños, the Philippines. The new varieties have a greater yield per acre, have shorter stalks (which makes them less susceptible to rotting due to heavy rainfall), and are more disease-resistant than other varieties. Unfortunately, this is an outstanding exception only, and falls short of the needs of the developing world today.

One example of untapped agricultural production potential is the hot humid area of tropical Latin America, where there are approximately two *billion* acres of undeveloped but potentially good crop land. Yet little or no research is being conducted in this area.

Despite the obvious need for trained agriculturists in the developing countries, very few students are sent to the United States to study *tropical* agriculture. The fault is not theirs, for not only does the United States have few courses to offer in tropical agriculture, but far too little is being done to encourage the expansion of centers for the study of agriculture. The means to provide training activity through the foreign aid program is an avenue not fully exploited, and the cultural exchange program is also a useful avenue little used. In order to expand our involvement in this vital area, both government and private industry in the United States should encourage and support our university agricultural research centers. If given additional support, the universities engaged in temperate-zone agricultural research could offer valuable scientific knowledge to developing countries.

Evidence of a decrease in the number of foreign students studying agriculture suggests that strong agricultural programs may become less rather than more available. "In nearly all Latin American countries for example," Thurston reports, "the percentage of university students studying agriculture has decreased during the past decade." He states that in Mexico the decline has been from 3 to 1 per cent; in Panama from 4 to 2 per cent and in the Dominican Republic, from 2 to 1 per cent. He points out that of 105,000 Latin American students enrolled in the United States during the decade 1956 to 1965, *only five per cent studied agriculture.*[6] Those agencies and organizations which send students to this country and other countries to study in the future should be urged to place special emphasis on the study of agriculture. It is no longer a question of whether or not the U.S. government should take a firmer stand on such matters; it now becomes a must if we are to get more mileage out of our foreign assis-

[6] Thurston, *Bioscience*, January 1969.

ance dollars and improve the agricultural production capacities of those who seek our assistance.

Research in tropical agriculture is not a panacea for the world food crisis which mankind now faces. However, in the long run it is in tropical agriculture that the big payoff will come when the underdeveloped areas of the world will be pressed for ever greater food supplies. The tremendous success of American agriculture today is a result of the combination of research, education, and extension in our land grant system of colleges and universities. A similar total effort in developing countries is seldom, if ever, found. Some of the difficulties faced in developing countries are largely due to a low priority given to agricultural education and technology—a most necessary ingredient for effective expansion of agricultural production. What many fail to realize is that the so-called take-off point in agriculture has been reached, but not in the tropics, the area most in need of knowledge about agriculture. Before a country can progress to industrialization, its urgent agricultural needs must be met. This is the issue before developing countries today. The cart (economic progress) cannot be placed before the horse (agriculture).

The task facing the developing countries is great and the effort required must be considerable, but the job can be done. I believe that the tools for implementing a massive and co-ordinated research and development program in tropical agriculture are available. With substantial self-help on the part of developing countries, our AID program, our universities, the UN, the FAO, the Peace Corps, private enterprise, and private foundations may substantially improve tropical agriculture in these countries. The President's Science Advisory Committee panel on world food supply and a 1964 MIT/AID International Conference on agriculture pointed out the urgent need to solve the food shortage problems of the developing world. What we now require is a massive co-ordinated effort, perhaps through government support of universities and foundations active in tropical agriculture. Properly co-ordinated and planned agricultural research in this country and in the major agricultural research centers elsewhere in the world, coupled with an emphasis on a far-reaching training program that would include administration and applied research, will contribute immeasurably to the economic progress of developing agricultural economies.

But agricultural research alone will not result in production gains without a co-ordinated plan for the locale which the research is focused upon. In the recent past there have been some notable successes in different parts of the world that provide a useful background to the agricultural development process. They are the Gezira Scheme in Sudan, the Comilla Project in East Pakistan, the JCRR in Taiwan, and Vicos in Peru. They serve to illustrate the importance of careful, co-ordinated planning based on the unique characteristics of the country involved. The nature of these four projects varies greatly, but in all of them, planners applied a packaged approach to development, an approach which took into account all the major factors involved in production—resources, institutional arrangements, rural sociology, and the like.[7]

The Gezira Scheme in the Sudan is one of the largest centrally managed agricultural operations in the world. It dates back to the early 1900's. Its purpose was to raise rural living standards and to provide the Sudanese government with revenues by utilizing the waters of the Nile for irrigation agriculture. The scheme is a joint venture and was originally financed by the British-controlled government of Egypt, a British-backed bond issue, and the Sudan Plantations Syndicate, a private company. Management is carried out by the company and by farmers' associations. Under its arrangement, the scheme provides for profit-sharing between the government, the company, and tenants, who are limited to 30 acres per family. Farmers devote one third of their acreage to long-

[7] The four projects are discussed briefly by Max Millikan and David Hapgood in *No Easy Harvest: The Dilemma of Agriculture in Underdeveloped Countries* (Boston: Little, Brown and Company, 1967), pp. 109–118.

staple cotton and the remainder to food and grain production, forage, and fallow. Planning is carried out by the company's management, and all phases of the operation—including credit, water allocation, seed, and extension—are closely supervised.

Gezira now has some 70,000 settlers and covers 1,800,000 acres. Of the scheme, Millikan and Hapgood stated:[8]

Gezira has succeeded where all too many irrigation schemes have failed. Its benefits have gone to most of the people in its area, rather than to the most skilled farmers. It has brought the benefits of large-scale estate management to peasant communities without sacrificing individual motivation. The settler's income is considerably higher than that of other Sudanese farmers. The scheme has repaid its costs and is now a major source of foreign exchange and development capital for the Sudanese government. Thus it benefits the nation as a whole, not merely the settlers.

The Comilla Project in East Pakistan combines comprehensive agricultural and extension services in a pilot project covering a rural population of about 150,000 in some 300 villages. It has grown out of the activities of the government's Academy for Rural Development and the Department of Agriculture. Its primary thrust was to overcome a severe lack of credit and deficiencies in extension and market organization among farmers in the area. One aspect of its success may be measured by the fact that, by 1964, production of its principal crop, rice, had increased to the point where East Pakistan, for the first time since Pakistan's independence, had a surplus of rice.[9] Included in the program are credit, farmer cooperatives, extension, flood control and water management, introduction of the use of fertilizer and machinery, and improved transport and marketing facilities.

[8] Ibid., p. 112.
[9] Akhter Hameed Khan, "The Comilla Project." Paper presented at Summer Study on Agricultural Productivity, Massachusetts Institute of Technology, July 13, 1964 (mimeo).

The Joint Commission for Rural Reconstruction (JCRR), in Taiwan, is an autonomous organization which grew out of a joint 1946–47 United States–Chinese study on productivity. Its aim was to increase agricultural productivity, improve rural living, and raise farm income. It views itself as a catalyst to stimulate rural development and growth, and its main focus is on agriculture. Production under JCRR programs doubled between 1952 and 1964. In the implementation of plans, JCRR has dealt through farmers' associations with all factors affecting productivity. Extension plays a large part in the dissemination of new information throughout Taiwan. United States aid has enabled the program to achieve rapid growth in the development of the physical and human infrastructure.

Under the JCRR program, irrigation doubled and fertilizer use was estimated at 750,000 tons annually by 1964. Marginal lands, both foothill land at elevations of 1,000 to 3,000 feet and tidal lands, are under development.

Vicos, in Peru, is a small community development project of anthropologists from Cornell University. In 1952, the University rented the 18,940-acre hacienda at Vicos, with the aim of starting the process of modernization to increase agricultural productivity among the hacienda's 1,800 inhabitants. After studying the community's needs, motivations, and social structure, the University introduced agricultural innovations tailored to the community. Through production of potatoes, the project became highly successful. In ten years, per-capita income rose from $40 to $250, as compared with the average in Peru of $179. In line with the Cornell plan, and on the intervention of Senator Edward Kennedy, the Peruvian government expropriated the project, which is now held communally and managed by an elected council.[10]

Examination of the various projects planned or executed through private investment and AID funds in agricultural

10 Millikan and Hapgood, pp. 115–116.

operations in underdeveloped areas shows that the projects are useful and add considerably to the production capacities and body of knowledge in the developing countries. The important shortcoming in these programs is that, with few exceptions, the projects are not in the vital area of research on tropical food or forage crops.

The world food supply panel's assessment of the funds needed for assistance to the developing countries in the area of technical assistance for food production is staggering in comparison to present levels. The need was estimated to be *$12 billion* annually for the 1965 base of capital investments expended in those seventy developing nations having food shortage problems. The need by about 1985 is expected to reach about *$25 billion* annually.

The world food panel said that "to achieve such a feat [improve agriculture production capacities in Asia, Africa, and Latin America] would require capital and technical involvement of developing and developed nations alike on a scale unparalleled in peace-time history of man." The present mood of the American people and the attitude of Congress are to reduce the amount of funds for technical assistance to developing countries. However, this mood and attitude are not in accord with the needs of the one half to two thirds of the rest of humanity who face mass starvation in the near future unless something is done to increase food supplies.

The chairman of the President's Science Advisory Committee panel on the world food supply enumerated three noble reasons for pursuing an unprecedented and massive effort in world food production: [11]

First, a humanitarian reason; second, a security reason—by the year 2000, there will be four times as many people in the developing countries as in the developed countries . . . the idea that security is more than military might is not new. Seneca, nearly

[11] Ivan L. Bennett, Jr., "Food and Population: An Overview," *Agriculture Science Review*, First Quarter 1968, pp. 10–17.

Economic Assistance by AID and Predecessor Agencies to Agriculture

(*In millions of dollars*)

	Obligations		
	Agriculture	Education	Health
1955	53.1	19.0	37.5
1956	68.0	25.8	34.2
1957	56.9	30.6	45.5
1958	75.4	33.9	51.5
1959	84.0	31.2	58.4
1960	203.7	44.4	48.8
1961	67.2	46.0	48.8
1962	118.8	91.1	59.0
1963	158.3	83.7	84.1
1964	127.5	69.4	67.3
1965	488.0	131.0	91.0
1967	561.2	137.4	125.9
1967	496.8	189.3	155.8
1968 (estimate)	569.3	198.9	194.6
1969 (estimate)	798.6	215.9	156.9

NOTE: Figures for assistance to agriculture, education, and health prior to fiscal year 1965 are not comparable with the assistance figures for that year and subsequent years. Prior to fiscal year 1965, AID assistance to these three sectors was recorded only for capital and technical project assistance. Program and sector loan assistance was included beginning in fiscal year 1965 to present a more accurate statement of AID activities in the New Initiative areas of agriculture, education, and health.

SOURCE: 90th Cong., 2d sess., House, *Hearings: Foreign Assistance and Related Agencies Appropriations for 1969, Part 2, Economic Assistance*, Washington, 1968, p. 414.

2000 years ago, warned the Roman Senate: "A hungry people listens not to reason nor is its demand turned aside by prayers." Third, a long range economic reason—an important way to expand our own economy in the future will be the creation of additional markets for U.S. foods and products.

The concept of greatly increased per-acre yields is relatively recent, even among developed nations. Rice yields in Japan rose slowly from about 1,750 pounds per acre in the sixteenth century to about 2,200 pounds in the nineteenth century, and then rose sharply with the application of modern technology after the turn of the century. A similar trend can be seen in the corn yields in the United States. From 1800 to about 1940 they were nearly static at 20 to 25 bushels per acre; with the introduction of hybrid varieties and through the use of other technologies yields have tripled, and in some instances quadrupled, in the past twenty-five years. The increases were made possible by the development and application of agricultural technologies, some of which had been known for many years. Even after extensive research, some crops have stubbornly resisted yield increases.

Any assumption that the technologies of developed nations can be quickly transferred to a given underdeveloped area is not sound. The achievements of the International Rice Research Institute in the Philippines have been due to intensive research over at least a quarter of a century, and further success with improved rice varieties will depend in large measure on the success of population programs, on carefully planned investment, and on adequate research adapted to the ecological, social, and economic conditions in underdeveloped regions. There are incontrovertible indications of the need to continue food aid programs and to promote international trading arrangements and policies enabling developing economies to maximize earnings from exports of their major products. Additional basic and adaptive research on agricultural productivity in many areas of the developing world, within the context of an integrated approach to over-all economic development, will be required on an international scale.

PART IV

Planning for the Future

9
What We Can Do

AFTER ATTEMPTING to define the dimensions of the population explosion, describe the problems it has created here and in the developing nations, and discuss difficulties and promising developments in the fields of birth control and agriculture, the next logical step is to determine what we as a nation and as individuals can do to slow the world population growth rate before it virtually destroys man. What must we do, in very practical terms, if our children and generations yet unborn are to have a future.

In a world whose population is doubling every thirty-five years, the keynote must be "action now." Admittedly, much research remains to be done for a long-term solution of the population problem; we need improved contraceptives and a fuller understanding of the social determinants of family size.

ACTION AT HOME

Our first step must be to launch a comprehensive attack on America's population problem. This would greatly enhance our chances of defeating a serious threat to the quality of life in this country. At the same time, it would set a positive example for the developing nations currently facing the prospect of famine and mass starvation, and demonstrate that our nation is willing to practice what we preach to others. For there are still many in the Third World who suspect our motives and view our international population programs with hostility.

Where do we begin? There are an estimated 4.3 million women in this country who *want* to practice family planning but either do not have access to or cannot afford proper medical assistance. Providing voluntary family-planning services to this group through public and private clinics and hospitals constitutes a top short-term priority.

Less than one fifth of all U.S. hospitals with large maternity services reported family-planning programs in 1966. Where better could a mother—particularly a poor young mother with an illegitimate child—receive instruction and the opportunity to avoid unwanted births than in the hospital after giving birth?

Doctors in those too few hospitals offering such services testify to their effectiveness and the enthusiastic response of their patients. In short, based on experience, we know that family-planning programs do work.

Private nonprofit organizations such as Planned Parenthood have established a number of successful family-planning clinics throughout the United States. But the task at hand is too large to rely on the private sector alone. Reaching the 4.3 million women who want assistance will require supplementing private efforts with a large-scale voluntary public family-planning program.

To date, public activity in the family-planning field has been timid and disorganized. The federal government devoted only $50 million in fiscal year 1969 to the solution of our national population problems. To make matters worse, this relatively meager sum was divided up among a large number of unco-ordinated agencies, none of which regards population or family planning as its primary focus.

The result is a scattering of small, generally ineffectual

population programs administered by the Children's Bureau, the Office of Education, the Office of Economic Opportunity, and the National Institute of Child Health and Human Development. The principal office created to deal specifically with the population problem, the office of the Deputy Assistant Secretary for Family Planning and Population in the Department of Health, Education, and Welfare, possesses *no* direct responsibility for any of these programs and is staffed by only two professionals in addition to the deputy assistant secretary.

That this fainthearted and fragmented effort with limited resources and no meaningful focus of action and responsibility has had little impact is no surprise.

Consolidating these disparate programs to provide uniform policy direction, co-ordination, and a system of accountability offers the most promising approach to the creation of an effective national program to eliminate and prevent unwanted births in America. Therefore, with the support of a large number of my colleagues in the Senate and the House of Representatives, I introduced legislation in the 91st Congress to establish a National Center for Population and Family Planning within the Department of Health, Education, and Welfare.

The functions of the proposed National Center would be to administer all population-related service and research programs currently scattered throughout HEW; to provide a liaison with population activities carried on by other agencies in the federal government; to provide training for the manpower needed to staff domestic and foreign population and family-planning services and research; and to be responsible for the evaluation of all population programs in HEW.

In addition, this legislation would require the Secretary of HEW to submit a five-year plan to Congress setting forth the guidelines and goals necessary to extend the family-planning services to all who desire them. Coupled with a systematic reporting system capable of yielding data on which service levels, cost estimates, and program evaluations could be based, the requirement of a multi-year plan would provide the comprehensive family-planning policy we now lack and desperately need.

However, reorganization of current family-planning programs alone is not enough. For present programs, even when taken together, lack sufficient scope. To successfully reach more than 4 million women we will have to greatly expand our delivery system for family-planning services.

This means more family-planning clinics, programs in hospitals, and, increasingly, the integration of family-planning services in a comprehensive voluntary maternal and child care program available to all American families. Accomplishing this will take money—more than the $50 million we are now investing in domestic family-planning services, research, and training. According to the President's Committee on Population and Family Planning chaired by John D. Rockefeller III and Wilbur Cohen, former Secretary of HEW, the initiation of a realistic domestic family-planning program will cost a minimum of $100 million in 1970, and substantially more in subsequent years.

To most of us, $100 million sounds like a staggering sum. But it is only 1/20 of 1 per cent of the federal government's budget for 1970, less than 2 per cent of the amount Americans legally bet on horse racing last year, less than 5 per cent of the unplanned excess production costs of a recent new Air Force cargo plane. As a nation with a gross national product about to top the trillion-dollar mark, we can certainly afford to invest $100 million in family planning. Indeed, if we wish to protect our affluence and unprecedented standard of living and preserve an environment fit for human habitation, we can scarcely afford *not* to make this relatively small investment in the future of our society.

We should also remember that resources expended on family-planning services and research yield real tax dividends. Experts both in and out of government have estimated that $1 spent providing family-planning services produces a reduction of $25 to $70 in the costs of public welfare, education, health, and housing programs. In other words, we are not talking about giveaway programs but rather an investment that will produce greater returns, dollar for dollar, than nearly any other public program in the United States.

Another critical issue relating to the problem of unwanted births in this country is abortion. Medically induced abortion is such a sensitive and controversial subject that there is an understandable tendency to simply avoid it and hope that the problem goes away by itself.

The fact is, it is not going away. Last year as many as 1.2 million American women may have had induced abortions to escape unwanted pregnancies. Unfortunately, only an estimated 5,000 to 10,000 of these met the legal criteria for a therapeutic abortion and were performed openly in hospitals under acceptable medical standards. The overwhelming majority took place surreptitiously, often under inexpert and unhygienic conditions which posed serious dangers to the lives and future health of the women involved.

Abortion in our society has traditionally been regarded as a matter of personal morality. How a person feels about the rightness or wrongness of abortion is determined by his conscience and religious values.

These differences in moral views about abortion have led to spectacular controversies in an increasing number of states, where reform of the laws which forbid any abortion has become an issue.

The need for reform, however, is unassailable. The startling, increasing statistics on illegal, unsafe, induced abortion tragically demonstrate that laws flatly forbidding any medically induced abortion have failed.

Similar to the liquor prohibition laws, the unyielding abortion laws have produced a vicious nation-wide illegal abortion racket which is growing year by year.

Laws which forbid voluntary abortion to women who

want them because of their physical or mental health, or defects in the fetus, raise enormous problems for our society which cannot be ignored. Reforming our present abortion laws accordingly should rank as a priority of any realistic and humane national family-planning policy.

So, in the short run, America's domestic population goal must be the elimination and prevention of unwanted births and the right of all parents to voluntarily plan the size of their families. Creating the national family-planning policy necessary to achieve this goal within the next five years is well within our capabilities.

But, in the longer run, we must look beyond family planning. For it is possible that our population will continue to expand at a dangerous rate even after the implementation of an effective national family-planning program because many parents will desire large families—will *plan* large families. We may discover, as one scientist put it, that we are "breeding ourselves into oblivion on purpose."

Ultimately, we will have to formulate a national population policy based on an inventory of our limited natural resources and a calculation of the number of people this country can support without sacrificing the quality of our institutions and environment. This policy would determine an optimum population size for the United States and provide noncoercive incentives to encourage birth rates consistent with the nation's best interests. As the situation is today, most economic and social incentives in this country—particularly our tax system—promote larger rather than smaller families.

Implementing a comprehensive population policy, however, will require a good deal more knowledge than we now have. Additional biomedical and contraceptive research is needed to develop a better birth control pill, one with no deleterious side effects and which does not demand daily attention. More importantly, behavioral research must be undertaken on a larger scale to discover the cultural and economic determinants of family size; that is, why a given family decides to have five children as opposed to one or two and what inducements could be created to affect a family's decision.

The success of a national population policy is predicated on informed responses to questions such as: What is our present stock of depletable natural resources and how long will it last at different population levels? How will the addition of 100 million more Americans over the next thirty years affect our daily lives and our environment? Will per-capita taxes have to double or triple in order to support an additional 100 million people? What is an optimum population size for a nation in America's circumstances and with America's aspirations for the future? So far, we can only guess at the answers.

Clearly, there is an urgent need for a great deal more population-related research. Out of a total budget of nearly $1 billion, the National Institutes of Health are devoting less than $10 million a year to research in this area. As Robert McNamara, president of the World Bank, put it: "Hundreds of millions of dollars for death control; scarcely 1 per cent of that amount for fertility control."

Finally, a national population policy will require the establishment of structures in the legislative and executive branches of the federal government capable of formulating and executing far-reaching population programs. Creating a Joint Standing Committee on Population and Human Environment would be a logical way to provide a source of expertise and a focus for legislative action in Congress. On the executive side, in time we will require a cabinet-level Department of Population and Environment to ensure the priority and attention the population problem deserves. Within the Executive Office of the President, a special assistant for population and environment would provide the necessary expertise in the White House.

In summary, in the United States we should:

1. Immediately reorganize and expand currently ineffectual public family-planning programs with the objective of grant-

ing all American parents the basic right to voluntarily plan the size of families.

2. Authorize the Secretary of HEW to submit a five-year national family-planning policy to Congress providing goals and guidelines for an ongoing campaign to eliminate and prevent unwanted births in this country.

3. Re-examine our coercive and barbaric abortion laws.

4. Greatly increase biomedical, contraceptive, and behavioral research in the population field.

5. Begin to lay the foundation for a national population policy to determine, based on an inventory of our resources and a vision of what we want America to become, how many people this nation can support without seriously compromising the quality of life and the environment for each of us.

6. Call for the establishment of a Joint Standing Committee of Congress on Population and Human Environment, a cabinet-level Department of Population and Environment and a Special Assistant to the President.

ACTION ABROAD

If mankind is to find a sane solution to the population problem on a global scale, America must assume a leadership role in this struggle. More than any other nation, we possess the technical know-how and material resources that are necessary components of any humane strategy to curb the world's soaring birth rate.

Our most pressing concern, of course, is to assist in buying time for those developing nations facing mass famine now and in the decades ahead. The giant U.S. food surpluses that saved millions in India and elsewhere from starvation in the 1960's are gone. Only crop yield increases and improved marketing techniques in those countries experiencing critical food shortages can avert disaster in the 1970's and 1980's.

Agricultural development in the tropical and subtropical areas of the world appeared to be hopelessly stagnating as recently as two or three years ago. However, the development of new strains of wheat and rice combined with more efficient production techniques has created a Green Revolution. In some areas of the world it has brightened the prospects for avoiding serious famine and for securing the time to implement a policy to stabilize world population growth. However, it is too early, admittedly, to say how widespread this revolution's impact will be. But there are enough encouraging signs to warrant our full support.

This means more money for research on new grain varieties, fertilizers, and methods of irrigation. We will also have to increase available loan funds to enable farmers in Asia, Africa, and Latin America to finance the mechanization which is the foundation of this potential increase in the earth's food supply. But we should never forget that, at best, this agricultural revolution is only a stopgap measure; it does not deal with the source of the problem, which is excessive population growth. If we are to avoid the tragedy of a world flooded with children who are born to starve, we must utilize every moment gained through increased crop yields to institute effective population programs to reduce birth rates drastically.

Moving quickly in the area of population planning is inherently difficult under the best of conditions; for even drastic population programs require several decades to take effect. The situation becomes next to impossible when the countries involved are not convinced that an effective population policy is essential to their development and, ultimately, their survival. And this is precisely the situation we are confronted with in the developing world today.

Many developing nations approach the question of population with dangerous misconceptions. If wide expanses of land exist, peopling it frequently is encouraged as an easy route to increased national power and wealth. What the governments of these nations fail to recognize is that land without capital in the twentieth century is worth little. Many of the newly emerged nations regard Western population control proposals as thinly veiled neocolonialist attempts at racial and national genocide designed to preserve global white supremacy. As a result, with the exception of a handful of countries such as Pakistan, India, and Taiwan, the great majority of the developing nations have refused to initiate policies to consciously regulate the size of their populations—and the population of the developing world continues to double at the incredible rate of once every twenty-five years.

Therefore, our first task on the international front must be to provide these governments with information that will convince them that establishment of national population policies is in their own best interests.

How do we accomplish it?

To begin with, population must be transformed into a more compelling and visible component of all economic assistance programs. Aid givers—whether single nations or international agencies—should stress the intimate interrelationship between population growth and economic development. Recipient countries must be encouraged to analyze their own population problems and to integrate family-planning and population programs into their long-term economic and social development plans.

The tools of persuasion will have to be the facts and tact. Insisting on the adoption of population policies as a condition for receiving economic assistance will only generate hostility and stiffen resistance. As the report of the Pearson Commission on International Development accurately perceived: "Development must come from within, and . . . no foreign help will suffice when there is no national will to make the fundamental changes which are needed."

In other words, effective efforts to stabilize population growth and reduce birth rates in the developing nations must be the product of conviction, not coercion. This is why it is imperative that we establish vigorous family-planning and population programs in the United States. We must demonstrate by our actions, not merely with words, that even the most affluent nation in the world recognizes the necessity of a population policy to protect its standard of living and promote its future development.

Another way to alleviate the resistance and suspicions of developing nations is to shift much of our population assistance from bilateral into multilateral channels. Bilateral aid arrangements create psychological obstacles which preclude effective use of economic assistance of any kind. And with an issue as sensitive and delicate as birth control, a nation-to-nation approach often presents difficult problems.

Successful foreign aid, the Pearson Commission concluded, must be closely linked to the economic objectives of aid receivers while at the same time permitting aid givers to ensure that their largess is not squandered; which is another way of saying foreign assistance cannot operate as a one-way street.

The commission's suggestion is greater reliance on multilateral aid structures:

The monitoring and assessment of performance is best done in a multilateral context in which donors and aid receivers jointly review the past and plan for the future. We attach great significance to the dialogue on aid performance and recommend that the World Bank and the regional banks take the lead in discussions leading to the extension of joint review procedures in consortia, consultive groups, or regional organizations, both those which now exist and those which need to be created.

This approach is particularly relevant to population-related assistance. I believe the United States could facilitate a move in this direction by specifically committing a larger portion of its population aid funds to multilateral development associations and special population trust funds administered by international organizations. An official American endorsement of the proposal to create a Commissioner for Population in the United Nations and promise of future financial backing for an expanded UN population program would constitute an important first step.

Another way to avoid the strictly government-to-government nature of our present aid efforts is through the development of a semi-autonomous government institute for overseas development assistance. It would, in the words of former Secretary of HEW John Gardner, create "a new kind of government research and development establishment" that would reproduce within the government structure "some of the more positive attributes of a nonprofit corporation." This type of institute, international in its scope, would remove the aid program from its total dependence on annual Congressional appropriations, encourage the American public to become more involved in overseas investment, and provide a much needed center for planning, research, and action in the area of foreign technical assistance. Population planning and agriculture, hopefully, would be the cardinal concerns of such an institute.

Finally, to an even greater extent than our domestic population programs, the progress of our international programs is dependent on achieving significant breakthroughs in contraceptive technology, biological and behavioral sciences. Birth control pills which must be taken daily and intra-uterine devices that require careful insertion and periodic checkups are simply not practicable in developing countries that are short on public health education and health facilities and long on superstition. In India, for example, a national campaign to reduce the birth rate through the massive distribution of IUD's was subverted by rumors that the loop was supposed to create alarming problems for couples, cause cancer, and swim through the bloodstream to the brain.

If the population problem is to be attacked on a global scale, more biomedical research must be undertaken to develop a contraceptive that is simple and effective enough for mass use in even the most backward societies. Only the more technologically advanced nations possess the resources and know-how to undertake such research.

And the problem in the developing nations is bigger than producing the perfect pill. Operational research is needed to help governments determine how to integrate population programs successfully into their society.

Fundamental values, societal mores, and institutional patterns are involved which often stand as obstacles to public campaigns to reduce birth rates. For instance, in nations without social insurance systems, people have large families for a valid economic reason: children are the principal means of support in old age. Any population policy in such a society that is not preceded by institutional changes which reduce dependence on the family as the sole source of security is bound to fail.

Thus, behavioral research on the links between family size and the social and economic functions of the family in a traditional society is a precondition for action in the population field in most developing countries.

Unfortunately, at this time we are not making enough resources available through our foreign assistance programs (AID) to support adequate population research. In 1969, AID spent only $50 million on all aspects, both services and research, of our international population program. More than $50 million could be justified for research alone. This is surely a case of being penny wise and pound foolish. I have introduced legislation in the Senate which would expand this sum considerably.

In summary, to serve as the catalyst for a global campaign to restore the growing imbalance between births and deaths, America should:

1. Support with U.S. funds and expertise the incipient agricultural revolution which offers the only hope for averting the starvation of millions of Asians, Africans, and Latin Americans in the next decade or two.

2. Place greater emphasis on our international population

efforts by creating an Assistant Secretary of State for Food and Population and an Assistant Administrator for Population in AID.

3. Channel more of our international population assistance through multilateral organizations such as the United Nations Population Trust Fund and specially created development consortia.

4. Ensure that we boast a vigorous domestic family-planning program as an example to less developed nations.

5. Provide the financial support for extensive biomedical, contraceptive and behavioral research in the population field.

6. Increase the appropriations for AID's population programs to $100 million in 1970 and considerably more in succeeding years.

TIME IS RUNNING OUT

As individuals, there are many things each of us can do. Grassroots activity is needed to inform Americans of the population problem and to mobilize public action in this area at the local, state, and national levels.

Civic groups must be convinced that family planning is an issue worth discussing with their membership. The media must be urged to dramatize the problem. Legislators can be informed by letter and personal visits that a large number of their constituents consider population a critical issue, an issue which could very well determine whom they vote for in the coming election.

Above all, we must create the tremendous sense of urgency the population problem demands. Change of every sort is occurring around us today with a breath-taking rapidity. This was graphically dramatized by H. G. Wells in his famous *Outline of History*. Wells suggested we consider the entire history of mankind in terms of twelve hours, with the present as the high noon of the long human day.

For the first eleven and a half hours nothing was recorded.

We know of no persons or events. We can only infer man was living on earth, for we find his stone tools and other archaeological remains.

Not until twenty minutes before twelve do the earliest vestiges of Egyptian and Babylonian civilization begin to appear. The Greek literature, science, and philosophy, which we call "ancient," are not seven minutes old.

At one minute before twelve the Mayflower lands at Plymouth. And not a half a minute has elapsed since man first began to make the steam engine do his work for him.

World War I began ten seconds ago.

The atom bomb fell on Hiroshima four seconds ago.

The first artificial earth satellite was launched two seconds ago.

Within the next five seconds we shall determine whether mankind will survive the population explosion. We must make a decision as individuals, as a nation, as a species to defuse the population bomb on which we are sitting, and we must make it soon.

If we act quickly, with resolution and imagination, we can bring our soaring population growth rates under control and concentrate on improving the lot of those who are born and are soon to be born. However, if we fail to act, the matter will soon be swept out beyond our reach. And the hands on H. G. Wells's clock of human history will suddenly stop. Then our children will indeed be "born to starve."

Index